The Pathet Lao

The Pathet Lao

Leadership and Organization

Joseph J. Zasloff

Lexington Books
D.C. Heath and Company
Lexington, Massachusetts
Toronto   London

Library of Congress Cataloging in Publication Data

Zasloff, Joseph Jermiah.
  The Pathet Lao: leadership and organization.

  1. Pathet Lao. I. Title.
DS557.L28Z37   322.4'2'09594   73-1068
ISBN 0-669-86744-6

Published simultaneously in Canada.

Printed in the United States of America.

International Standard Book Number: 0-669-86744-6

Library of Congress Catalog Card Number: 73-1068

Contents

List of Figures

Abbreviations

DRV	Democratic Republic of Vietnam (North Vietnam)
FAR	Forces Armées Royales (Royal Lao Armed Forces)
FBIS	Foreign Broadcast Information Service
ICC	International Control Commission
ICP	Indochinese Communist Party
LPLA	Lao People's Liberation Army (Kongthap Potpoi Pasason Lao)
NLFSV	National Liberation Front of South Vietnam
NLHS	Neo Lao Hak Sat (Lao Patriotic Front)
NVA	North Vietnamese Army
NVN	North Vietnam
PL	Pathet Lao (Land of the Lao; by extension, various components or the totality of the Lao revolutionary movement)
PPL	Phak Pasason Lao (People's Party of Laos)
RLG	Royal Lao Government

Preface

The cease-fire in Laos agreed to on February 21, 1973, has brought a welcome interruption to the large-scale violence. However, the struggle in Laos, as in Vietnam, has been over the question of who would rule the country, and that question has remained unresolved. The cease-fire does not bring an end to the political struggle—indeed, it focuses attention upon it. Little study has been devoted to one of the participants in this struggle, the Lao revolutionary movement, commonly referred to as the Pathet Lao ("Land of the Lao," or PL). This book aims at contributing to an understanding of the political dynamics of the Pathet Lao, analyzing its leadership, its commanding party (the People's Party of Laos), its front (the Lao Patriotic Front), its political and administrative organizations, and its military forces.

This study draws upon a series of interviews conducted by the author and a colleague during eight months of residence in Laos during 1967. Lao who had participated jointly with current Pathet Lao (PL) leaders in the early nationalist movement, the Lao Issara, gave interesting recollections of the origins and development of the subsequent Pathet Lao revolutionary organization. Certain Royal Lao Government (RLG) officials who had confronted PL leaders across the conference table or had served with them in Vientiane during several periods of coalition government—and in some cases had been schoolmates and friends, or were linked to them by family ties—offered useful insights about PL personalities and policies. Interviews with Pathet Lao and North Vietnamese prisoners and defectors were valuable in helping us to understand the contemporary movement. (A list of those interviewed may be found in Appendix H.) Specialists on Laos of many nationalities, including scholars, journalists, officials of international agencies, and foreign governmental officials were interviewed, and a variety of Pathet Lao documents, including party directives and training instructions, textbooks, propaganda, and general literature were examined.

In addition, this study is based upon a body of more recent information, including a systematic examination of PL radio broadcasts and published materials as well as statements on Laos emanating from Hanoi, Moscow, and Peking. In Washington the research has included a study of current reports of Pathet Lao and Vietnamese prisoners and defectors, refugee interviews, and translations of recently captured Pathet Lao and North Vietnamese internal documents. Finally, the small body of contemporary scholarly, governmental, and journalistic literature on Laos was, of course, consulted. Although the bulk of the research was completed in 1971, the author visited Laos twice in 1972 while a Fulbright professor in Southeast Asia and was able to verify and update the text.

The author expresses his gratitude for the valuable assistance he received from friends and colleagues in the preparation of this volume. Earlier drafts received careful criticisms and abundant suggestions from Paul F. Langer. Stephen T. Hosmer and Douglas Blaufarb gave their time generously in stimulating discussions and criticizing several chapters. Written comments were supplied on various chapters by Melvin Gurtov, Hans Heymann, Konrad Kellen, Robert Solomon, Mark S. Pratt, Peter Lydon, and James Murphy. Tela C. Zasloff provided generous research and editorial assistance. Finally, the author wishes to acknowledge the support given this work by the Rand Corporation under its program of research for the Advanced Research Projects Agency of the Department of Defense. Those organizations and persons to whom I am indebted for assistance do not necessarily share the views expressed in this study.

Joseph J. Zasloff

1

The Pathet Lao Leadership[a]

The Lao Context

Political power in Laos has never been monolithic or geographically concentrated. Prior to the French colonial domination, power was divided among the various ruling houses, hereditary mandarins, village headmen, and tribal chieftains. Although colonial rule introduced a new set of decision makers—the French and their Vietnamese helpers—and created some semblance of a quasi-modern administration, the traditional power structure, particularly outside of the capital, remained important. Indeed, families with a traditional base of power found favor in the colonial administration, and their sons were educated in the French schools. Thus, the elite of postcolonial Laos still tend to be drawn from this group.

Much of this traditional pattern remains in the Pathet Lao (PL) movement. Some leaders derive prominence from their roots in the noble or otherwise prominent families of the country. A few of these—Prince Souphanouvong is the most striking example—have national prominence. Others, whose families have claimed fealty from local residents over generations, have a more limited geographic base. Some derive their influence as chieftains of tribes or ethnic groups. Historical circumstances have brought these leaders with traditional status in Lao society into the Communist movement, and they continue to hold important positions. The fact that traditional bases of power are still important should not obscure the growing significance of "modern" institutions—the party, the army, the administration, and the front—as new bases of political power. Still another source of power within the Pathet Lao, perhaps the most important though clearly not the exclusive one, has been the favor of the Vietnamese Communists. Particularly for those individuals who did not have the advantages of birth and family connections, it is clear that support from Hanoi has been essential to their prominence.

In stressing the traditional, the institutional, and the foreign bases of power in the Pathet Lao movement, we do not mean to ignore the importance of personal qualities. Clearly, there is latitude within the Pathet Lao context for the particularly clever, ambitious, energetic, and politically talented men to maneuver. Indeed, in each of the categories of leadership we have suggested, the

---

[a]A brief historical sketch, providing a background of the Pathet Lao movement, a discussion of the emergence of the PL leadership, and profiles of three important PL personalities, is presented in Appendix A.

personal characteristics of an individual must be considered, in addition to his source of support, to explain his rise to the top. Some men have the gift of acquiring political power, others do not.

Although Pathet Lao leadership is considerably more cohesive than that of their Royal Lao Government (RLG) opponents, it is nevertheless difficult to identify with certainty the full membership of the Pathet Lao "ruling elite" or to rank in order of importance those who are identified. Contributing to this difficulty is the secrecy of the ruling party, which does not reveal membership in its ruling organs. The few journalists who have gained access to the Pathet Lao capital have not written analytically about the leadership structure, partly because to our knowledge no outside observer (with the exception of Vietnamese) has ever enjoyed an opportunity for continuous and intimate association. Reports by Soviet, Chinese, Japanese, or French visitors to the zone generally tell us little about the interrelationships among the Pathet Lao elite and about their character and orientation. Furthermore, the environment of Laos makes it inevitable that there will be a relative diffusion of power at this stage of development, despite the Communist institutions and attempts under Vietnamese guidance to increase the central authority. Populations are highly diverse, and certain local leaders continue to exercise an important measure of authority. Most regions are mountainous and sparsely populated; there are few roads; communications are poor; continuous warfare and particularly the very heavy U.S. bombings have further disrupted intrazonal communications and complicated the Communist leadership's efforts to create a centralized and effective authority. The embryonic political and administrative institutions are limited in their capacity to mobilize and regulate such varied peoples under a centralized leadership. Decisions cannot be dictated at headquarters and swiftly executed throughout the Communist zone. Finally, over the past two decades of Lao Communist activity, various leaders have moved in and out of prominence, depending upon the roles they perform, the particular instruments they control, and the intensity of Vietnamese support they have enjoyed at particular stages of Lao history. Despite the problems in identifying and ranking the Lao Communist leaders, we know enough about their background and activities over the past two decades to present hypotheses about their group characteristics.

Attributes of Pathet Lao Leadership

Our analysis has drawn upon biographical information about twelve leaders who are probably among the leading policy makers of the Lao Communist movement today.[b] These are leaders about whom we have been able to gather the most data, although still incomplete and possibly inaccurate in some specific elements.

---

[b]These leaders are: Faydang, Kaysone Phomvihan, Khampay Boupha, Khamtay Siphandone, Nouhak Phongsavan, Phoumi Vongvichit, Phoun Sipraseut, Singkapo Chounramany, Sisana Sisane, Sithon Kommadam, Souk Vongsak, and Souphanouvong.

All have been members of the resistance for more than twenty years and could appropriately be called "founding fathers" of the PL movement. All are members of the Central Committee of the Neo Lao Hak Sat (NLHS), or Lao Patriotic Front, and are thought to be members of the People's Party of Laos (PPL) although, since membership lists are not published, this cannot be verified. (The PPL is discussed in Chapter 2.) All are mentioned frequently in current NLHS radio and press releases. However, although these leaders are important we cannot be absolutely certain that they are indeed the only key policy makers.

We have more limited data about other prominent Pathet Lao personalities and, when the nature of the observation permits, our generalizations will go beyond the dozen leaders of our sample. It should be clear that in view of the paucity of available data we are not attempting to analyze this sample in any rigorous statistical sense. Rather we are mining our information about their backgrounds for insights into the qualities of the Pathet Lao leadership.

Longevity in the Movement

Prince Souphanouvong, born in 1909, appears to be the oldest of the top PL policy makers. On July 13, 1969, his birthday was celebrated "jubilantly," according to the Pathet Lao radio[1] in the PL zone, marking twenty-five years that the prince had served in the revolutionary activities, starting out at age thirty-five. Faydang, an ethnic minority leader, is only one year his junior. Sithon, another ethnic minority leader, is also one year Souphanouvong's junior (although another report puts Sithon's year of birh at 1906). Phoumi Vongvichit ranks among the older members, his birthdate being given variously as 1914, 1910, and 1909, and Nouhak is in the same age range, having been born in 1914 or 1910.

Kaysone, probably born in 1925 (although another report puts it at 1920), is one of the youngest of the founding fathers; he would have been twenty years old when he first entered the resistance in 1945. Khamtay Siphandone is a year younger, having been born in 1926. In 1970, the others were in their late forties or early fifties (Souk Vongsak, born about 1915; Sisana Sisane, 1922; Singkapo, 1913; Phoun Sipraseut, 1920; and Khamphay Boupha, 1917). It is striking that these men have been working in the Lao revolutionary movement for nearly a quarter of a century, i.e., most of their adult lives. There is considerable social diversity among them, yet as we shall presently point out service together over so many years, often in danger and adversity, has forged a unity and common philosophy. Their longevity in the Communist movement has also given these leaders a deep investment in the triumph of their cause.

Their long involvement with foreign allies over the years has been significant in the education of their children. As their children reach the age of secondary education, or even primary in some cases, the PL leaders are obliged to look outside of Laos, since quality education is even now not available in their zone. They have availed themselves of the opportunities open to them in North Vietnam, Communist China, and the Soviet Union and, for a few, in Eastern European Communist countries. Of Prince Souphanouvong's ten children, five have studied in Moscow and Eastern Europe and others in Communist China; Faydang, whose four wives gave him at least fourteen children, sent several to school in North Vietnam and Communist China; Souk Vongsak was reported to have one son in Moscow in 1955 and two sons and two daughters in Communist China in 1959. Phoumi Vongvichit was also reported to have children studying in Moscow and Communist China. As a consequence, the ties of these leaders to the Communist countries have been drawn tighter and their inclination to compromise with their Royal Laos Government adversaries who have been similarly drawn into the non-Communist orbit—primarily France, Thailand, and recently the United States—is reduced.

In conversations with Lao whose families are divided as a result of the war, we sensed the personal and political implications of having one's children educated in the Communist countries. A former PL official (A-24),[c] for example, who had remained on the RLG side after the integration agreements of 1957 told us that he sent his son to study in Peking, along with the children of Souphanouvong, after the Geneva Agreements in 1954. His son completed secondary school there, continued on with higher education in agriculture, and returned in 1962 to Khang Khay, where the Pathet Lao and neutralists were stationed at the time. There the young man found an opportunity to study medicine in North Vietnam and left for the University of Hanoi, where he was still a student in 1967. Our interviewee, now a judge in an RLG provincial town, learned that his son had been criticized in Hanoi because his father was collaborating with the "puppet government." He had letters from his son until 1964, but since then he has had no direct news. Since that year of the rupture of PL relations with the tripartite government, he has not seen his only other child, a daughter who is married to a Deuanist neutralist officer and lives with her husband in the Pathet Lao-controlled zone in Khang Khay. In the judge's words, "They have my two children. That's the reason I can't talk too much." As a sad afterthought to this observation, the judge added:

Of course, if my son came back, what would he do here? He knows Vietnamese and Chinese, but not French or English. If he comes out to this side without the capacity that people have here, what kind of position would he have? Perhaps he could make a go of it in the army, but in a civilian function what would he be able to do?

Ethnic Composition

Like their adversaries on the non-Communist side, the principal leaders of the Lao Communist movement are with a few exceptions lowland Lao (Lao Loum).

[c]Designation in parentheses used above and hereafter refers to Appendix H, Selective List of Persons Interviewed or Consulted.

This is not surprising, despite the fact that they rule the highland areas where tribal minorities predominate. The Lao Communist movement, as part of the larger nationalist movement in Laos, had its beginnings among the lowland Lao most affected by "modern" trends in the Mekong Valley towns, particularly in the secondary schools. The relative homogeneity in religion, language, and culture of the lowland Lao, as contrasted with the variegated highland minorities, made it more likely that a small, western-educated, town-based leadership would organize the nationalist movement, comparatively mild as it was in Laos. The highland minorities were the most backward peoples of Laos whose tribal chieftains had almost no modern education and, with some exceptions we have noted, were unlikely to produce many nationalist leaders.

Although the veteran PL leaders are principally lowland Lao, many have close personal and family relationships with the Vietnamese and most speak Vietnamese. A number, including Souphanouvong, Nouhak, and Singkapo, have Vietnamese wives. Kaysone's father is Vietnamese. Many, like Souphanouvong, Kaysone, and Sisane, were educated in Vietnam or, like Nouhak, had other lengthy residence in Vietnam even before 1945. After the hostilities began in 1946, and especially after their own headquarters and "Resistance Government" were established in North Vietnam, they all had frequent occasion to serve or visit in Vietnam. Even within Laos there were many occasions for developing Vietnamese relationships, since the towns generally numbered more Vietnamese than Lao inhabitants. The commercial and administrative contacts with Vietnam were most active in the southern panhandle of Laos, where the towns of Thakhek (Singkapo's birthplace), Savannakhet (birthplace of Kaysone, Nouhak, and Sisana), and Pakse (birthplace of Phoun Sipraseut and Khamtay Siphandone) were linked to Hue and Tourane over the short distances by the east-west colonial roads. It is not surprising that many Lao youngsters growing up in these towns developed a familiarity with and, in some cases, an attachment for things Vietnamese.

While the Pathet Lao organization has been dominated by lowland Lao since its origins, it is important not to overlook the several ethnic minority leaders who were charter members of the revolutionary movement. Sithon Kommadam, of Alak-Loven stock from southern Laos, is the most prominent leader from the Lao Theung. Another Lao Theung (though he was raised by a Lao family), who has been at the second echelon of PL leadership from the outset, is Apheui Keobounheuang, born in Savannakhet Province in 1915. Apheui was a member of the original "Resistance Committee of the East" and in 1956 was appointed to the NLHS Central Committee, on which he still serves. There are at least three more Lao Theung on the current Central Committee of the NLHS who were named to that body as early as 1956: Am Lo and his brother Am Vu of Savannakhet (both reported to be PPL members) and Ba Noi of Muong Sing (said to be a Central Committee member of the PPL). In addition, May Kham Di, a Tai Lu from Nam Tha, was also a member of the NLHS Central

Committee (and reportedly a PPL member) until his assassination in 1959.

The Meo have been represented in the PL leadership from its beginning by Faydang and his younger brother Nhia Vu as well as by Lo Foung Pablia. There have been frequent reports that Faydang does not carry real weight in policy-making circles but has been maintained in public prominence because of his long-time identification by the Lao Communist movement as a great Meo leader. Two other Meo who appear to be current members of the NLHS Central Committee are Lao Phong and Phiahom Sombat.

Despite the domination of the Lao Communist movement by lowland Lao leaders, we have the distinct impression that the PL have been more successful in mobilizing ethnic minorities (with the possible exception of the Meo) into their movement than have their RLG competitors. Sithon Kommadam, descendant of a prominent anti-French tribal leader, had great appeal among a number of the highland tribes in southern Laos based upon traditional and personal factors, and he was instrumental in bringing a significant number under Pathet Lao authority. Since the principal PL geographic focus has been in the mountainous areas, most heavily populated by ethnic minorities, the PL leaders have found it useful to show sensitivity to the special ethnic interests. They have received guidance in the development of an ethnic doctrine from the North Vietnamese, who had been astute in building their own revolutionary movement within the mountain minorities of Vietnam and parts of Laos and have continued to show unusual competence in managing these groups.[2] Since the Democratic Republic of Vietnam (DRV) contains most of the same mountain peoples in even greater numbers than does Laos, Vietnamese advisers are familiar with these ethnic groups and can offer experienced guidance for their rule. It seems likely that the domination by lowland Lao leaders within the Lao Communist movement will be gradually modified as Lao Theung and Lao Soung students who have been selected for education in North Vietnam, China, and the Soviet Union return to the zone and reach maturity.

Social Class, Education, and Occupational Background

The veteran PL lowland Lao leaders came from two broad categories of social backgrounds: noble or prominent families, who acquired as a birthright a measure of prestige and connections within Lao society, and more modest origins, generally in the towns. The first group, which included Prince Souphanouvong, Prince Souk Vongsak, Phoumi Vongvichit, and Singkapo Chounramany, normally attended one of the French lycées in Indochina. Souphanouvong appears to be the only PL leader who has completed the university. (Although Kaysone attended the Faculty of Medicine at Hanoi, he apparently did not complete his course.)

It is not surprising that some upper-class nationalists choose the Communist movement during a period of revolutionary struggle. Indeed, Asian Communist parties generally, including the Lao Dong party of the DRV, have been dominated by upper- and middle-class leaders.[3] However, since these PL leaders would have had the social attributes for mobility if they had remained with their upper-class Issara colleagues, their choice of joining forces with the Vietnamese Communists is interesting. We have already discussed, in an earlier study, Prince Souphanouvong's motives in joining forces with the eastern group, allied with the Vietnamese.[4] Some men were attracted by the force of his personality and followed him. Certainly they saw themselves as patriots, fighting to expel the French, and did not share the apprehension of the Vietnamese which their Issara colleagues felt. Some may have felt that their career mobility would be greater on the eastern side, recognizing that the competition from others with equal social status would be less than in Vientiane. Others may have found themselves on the eastern side by pure happenstance or simply luck (or ill luck).[d]

The leaders linked to the eastern group came mostly from modest social backgrounds, without the family connections for ascribed high rank within traditional Lao society. These men, with the exception of Kaysone, generally had even less formal schooling than did the upper-class group. However, one should not underestimate the amount of self-education acquired by most of these veteran leaders, whether or not they had much schooling. For example, many have mastered several foreign languages. A case in point is Sisana Sisane who was later to be working in the field of PL cultural affairs and propaganda. Though he completed only a Lao primary education in Savannakhet, he learned to speak Thai, Vietnamese, and French fluently. These tongues may have come naturally in the course of his career as a commercial traveler between Laos and Thailand, a policeman in Savannakhet between 1942 and 1944, and a customs guard at Savannakhet from 1944 to 1945.

It seems reasonable to conjecture that the veteran PL leaders from modest social backgrounds initially felt less attraction to remain with the Issara movement than did their upper-class colleagues, knowing there would be less interest in their talents in Vientiane where success and promotion were largely determined by educational and social qualifications. Moreover, they had fewer social connections that would draw them into the upper-class Issara circles. For many in this group, connections with Vietnamese sponsors proved more important to their careers (although rendering them vulnerable to the charge that they are serving foreign interests).

---

[d]We are inclined to give greater weight to the factor of chance in Lao politics than to many important factors that obtain elsewhere, such as ideology. An interview we had with a neutralist colonel, though it deals with the events of a different political faction in 1960, helps to make this point. Seriously examining how he became committed to the Kong Le faction, he admitted that he had been a regular officer in the Royal Army (Forces Armées Royales, or FAR), caught as a bystander in a fire fight in Vientiane in 1960, and given protection by some Kong Le officers. He struck up a friendship with them and, though he insisted he had no strong political inclination at the time, he decided to join them on their flight to the Plain of Jars. In the months that followed, he developed close personal ties with them, and he has remained identified as a "neutralist colonel," though it is difficult to determine what neutralism means in his personal ideology.

An Assessment

The continuity of the veteran leadership is remarkable, the group having remained virtually intact for more than two decades of intermittent war and coalition government. This longevity of service has not meant that as a group they are especially elderly, since they began their revolutionary careers as young men. It is clear that there is also an unusual cohesion within the leadership that has permitted them to serve over two decades with no evidence of major purges or defections. This unit, in sharp contrast with the factionalism of the RLG elite, impels one to search for the sources.

Perhaps the most important tie that holds them together is their common experience in the revolutionary struggle, creating that camaraderie of fighting men which is so often a powerful unifying force. An RLG study of the NLHS, prepared in the late 1950s, astutely recognized this bond:

The real link which binds the members of the NLHS is the memory of years of fighting together and the feeling that they must stick together so that those difficult years will not have been in vain. Those years were hard, full of real sacrifices and sufferings; they must not be wasted. Only unity and advancement of the NLHS can bring its members the position and the advantage to which they consider themselves entitled.

No doubt these leaders have had a full measure of danger and adversity, though there have been years of relative calm as well. They were harassed and pursued by the French in the first Indochina war from 1946 to 1954. Although there was little physical danger from 1954 to 1959, the political contention continued unabated and, in 1959, sixteen key leaders languished in prison for almost a year. Violence broke out from 1960 to 1962 and was converted once again to a political struggle from 1962 to 1963. Following the rupture of relations in the tripartite government in 1963 and the flight of Pathet Lao leaders to their zone in eastern Laos, living conditions once again became primitive for them. Many of the headquarters in which they worked were located in large caves to protect them from frequent bombardment, and there was constant danger to their lives from air attack. Their housing was rudimentary and food supplies were limited. The PL zone depended for manufactured consumer supplies upon shipments from Communist China and North Vietnam, neither of which, understandably, was lavish with its resources. However, judging from the development of the RLG, it seems to be the contrary conditions of relative comfort and luxury, abundant food and security, which contribute to factionalizing a group.

There are other reasons for PL cohesion. They are linked by a common cause which they have served for more than twenty years. The Marxist-Leninist ideology that they profess has probably made less mark upon them than have their common goals and sense of shared patriotism. One can also find a partial explanation for their cohesion in their developing institutions. Following the

Communist model of their DRV mentor and with active Vietnamese guidance they have constructed a ruling party and a front which help keep them together. These are in addition to the such institutions also possessed by their RLG competitor as an administration and an army. They have constructed a system of indoctrination and self-criticism which contributes to the unity. The presence of a unified Vietnamese Communist structure within the disparate Lao groups has also helped to keep the PL leadership on a steady course. Finally, the North Vietnamese model of cohesiveness and high morale in the face of interminable hardship has been a source of inspiration.

The bonds of unity were tested against many opportunities to leave the movement, especially the intermittent unions and disunions with the Royal Lao Government since the founding of a separate Pathet Lao organization in 1950. Only after the integration agreement of 1957 did a handful of second-level leaders quit. Perhaps it is not such a matter of wonderment that the PL leaders did not defect to the other side. Their personal investment—their authority, their careers, their personal lives, and the welfare of their families—has been so bound up with the Lao Communist movement that it was probably not within their realistic choice to abandon it. It is instructive to look back at earlier RLG assessments of certain PL leaders whom they believed to be prone to rally to the RLG because of "bourgeois" tastes—Singkapo was frequently cited—or lack of Communist ideological commitment, or strong family ties within the RLG zone. None of the leaders defected. Instead, political distance of the PL leaders from their RLG adversaries widened in recent years with the intensification of the war. The stress to which they were subjected did not break their morale—it seems to have strengthened their resolve. These comments are not meant to imply that the PL leaders may not find common ground with the RLG elite. There is a pull toward reconciliation that derives from family and sentimental ties and the common bonds of Lao patriotism. However, embitterment on both sides increased as the scope of the war in Laos widened, making such reconciliation difficult. Moreover, leaders on both sides have leaned more heavily upon their foreign supporters: the Pathet Lao upon the DRV and, to a lesser extent, Communist China and the Soviet Union; the RLG upon the United States and, to a lesser extent, Thailand. Thus, as the interests of the Lao leaders became involved in the complicated web of foreign interests, unity within Laos grew even more difficult to achieve.

2 The People's Party of Laos

Most nations at the lower end of the developmental scale have few of the modern political instruments such as parties or mass organizations. To rule, their leaders rely principally upon personal authority, executing the minor tasks of government largely through the civilian and military bureaucracies. The principal form of political controversy in the central government is the struggle for power among the elites, often carried out without much regard for the larger population. Governmental leaders in the capital normally devote little effort to organizing politically the country dwellers who, in turn, are little concerned with the central government. Local control continues to reside, in an important measure, with such regional elites as local satraps, military officers, and tribal chiefs; to exert influence in the various regions, leaders at the center must negotiate with these regional elites.

The Royal Lao Government, following this pattern, is directed by upper-class, lowland Lao civilian and military elites who depend for the execution of policy upon a small, poorly trained and poorly paid bureaucracy and upon the officers of the 55,000 to 75,000 military force (the Forces Armées Royales, or FAR), largely developed since 1954. To control some of the ethnic minority groups such as the Meo, these elites rely upon tribal leaders with whom they have made tenuous alliances. The RLG identifies with Theravada Buddhism and the king in Luang Prabang, symbols that exert a strong appeal to the population of the Mekong Valley in the northern segment of Laos. However, in the south, the former royal house of Champassak, currently led by Prince Boun Oum, still attracts the primary loyalty, and in other regions the sons of former ruling families have important local influence. Conflict among elite factions is rife, but the rural population has been largely unaware of and unaffected by the factional struggle in Vientiane. The most important associations have been formed around a few powerful families, whose branches often develop widespread relationships. However, the RLG elites have not developed any sustained, national political organizations.

By contrast, the Pathet Lao leadership, with North Vietnamese guidance, has been developing a set of relatively modern political instruments to mobilize and control the rural inhabitants. This is noteworthy in view of the less-developed aspects of the PL zone. The population is more diverse, with large numbers of highland minorities who speak many languages. The PL zone is also more backward economically, with widespread use of a dry-rice method of cultivation instead of the more advanced wet-rice methods of the lowlands. Indeed, in most aspects of modernity, in roads, towns, and electricity, for example, the PL areas lag behind the RLG regions. However, in constructing a ruling party, which we shall discuss presently, and such other institutions as a political front and mass organizations, to be described in the following chapter, the PL leaders have introduced entirely new notions and forces into traditional Laos.

Origins and Development

In 1930, Vietnamese Communist revolutionaries led by Ho Chi Minh founded the Indochinese Communist party (ICP), which declared its task to be "to wipe out feudal remnants, to distribute land to the tillers, to overthrow imperialism and to make Indochina completely independent."[1] The formation of the ICP consolidated three Vietnamese Communist factions that, according to a DRV history, had "indulged in invective against each other and disputed for influence among the masses."[2] The Communist International, learning of this, sent the Vietnamese revolutionary leader Ho Chi Minh to Hong Kong to unify the factions into a single party. At first, this new party gave itself the name, "Vietnam Communist Party." Once again, the Communist International sent instructions that were adopted, this time to change the party's name to Indochinese Communist Party because "the Vietnamese, Cambodian, and Laotian proletariats have politically and economically to be closely related in spite of their difference in language, customs, and race."[3] It appears that the Comintern was displeased by the nationalist tone of the name Vietnam Communist Party and preferred the broader, more internationalist scope implicit in the new name.[4]

Since the ICP's stated purpose was to liberate Laos and Cambodia as well as Vietnam, it is interesting that there were apparently no Lao or Cambodian members in this organization at the outset.[5] The Vietnamese Communists maintained the ICP as an almost exclusive Vietnamese party, at least in regard to Laos, for the duration of its formal existence until 1945 when, to camouflage its Communist connections, it was declared dissolved (though it continued as an "underground" party).

After 1945, as the Vietnamese Communists launched a vigorous organizational effort, it appears that they recruited a small number of Lao members into the ICP. Despite their preoccupation with Vietnam, particularly in the years from 1945 to 1950 when they were constructing their own revolutionary organization, the Vietnamese enlisted some Lao in the effort to expel the French. For example, the half-Vietnamese Kaysone Phomvihan was apparently recruited into the ICP when he was a student in Hanoi in 1946 or early 1947, and Nouhak, who was engaged in a trucking business in Vietnam, joined in 1947.

In early 1951, actions by the Vietnamese prepared the ground for the later formation of a separate Lao Communist party. In February of that year at a party congress the Vietnamese Communists proclaimed the formation of the

Vietnamese Workers Party (Dang Lao Dong) to replace the ICP. Eliminating the "Indochinese" label of the Communist party seemed designed to appeal to nationalist sentiments in Vietnam, Laos, and Cambodia. The Vietnamese organizers of this congress, with the aim of demonstrating close links among the three peoples, invited a number of Cambodian and Lao leaders to attend. Immediately following this Lao Dong party congress, and perhaps at the very same location, there was announced the formation of a Viet-Lao-Khmer alliance that committed these three peoples to struggle jointly against French colonial power and the "American interventionists."[6] No public announcements were made regarding the formation of separate Lao and Cambodian Communist parties; however, the purpose of publicizing this alliance was apparently to reinforce the image of an independent Lao and Cambodian revolutionary effort against the French.

Although there are still gaps in our knowledge about the specific form of Lao Communist party activity during the period from this proclamation in February 1951 until March 22, 1955, when the People's Party of Laos (Phak Pasason Lao) was formally announced, and there are some contradictory reports, we can piece together enough bits of information to offer an interpretation of events surrounding the establishment of the Lao Communist apparatus.

A Lao governmental study states that in 1952 a section of the Lao Dong party responsible for Laos was created under the name of Phak Khon Ngan (Labor Party). In 1953, after a "purification" ("cette section épurée") that left seventeen full members and a number of candidate members, the section was made independent and became, under the same name (Phak Khon Ngan) the ruling Lao Communist party. According to this study, the Lao Communist party grew, with the DRV maintaining its control through these seventeen Lao plus the candidate members, who held joint membership in the Lao Dong party. This explanation was adopted and appeared in U.S. governmental reports as well as the open literature until recently.[7]

We have discussed in an earlier study what we believe are mistakes in this explanation.[8] Briefly, there probably was no such Lao party called the Phak Khon Ngan (this term is a translation into Lao of the term Dang Lao Dong, meaning Workers Party), and we believe that the Vietnamese have been using a different method, principally their advisory system, to guide their Lao junior partners. In finding fault with this explanation, however, we do not reject the probability that Lao members of the Lao Dong party became important leaders of the Lao Communist party by reason of their close links to the Vietnamese Communists, their longevity in the revolutionary movement, and other attributes we have discussed. In fact, we have uncovered new information (since our earlier study) that confirms the importance of the former Lao members of the ICP in the creation of the People's Party of Laos (PPL).[9]

Discussing the origins of the PPL, a party training document (LP-24)[a] tells of

---

[a]Designations in parentheses used above and hereafter identify PL documents located in our files.

the decision of the Second General Assembly of the ICP in 1951 to dissolve itself into three parties in order "to conform to the plan for the expansion of the revolutionary struggle in each country" (Vietnam, Cambodia, and Laos). The document continues:

After that, the Lao who were members of the [Indochinese] Communist Party led the Lao people in their continuing struggle.
Though it had been organized and expanded some time before, the PPL was proclaimed on 22 March 1955. Based on these facts, it can be said that the PPL, as the successor of the ICP, still carries out the tasks of that party.

This interpretation is reinforced by an account in the RLG newspaper *Xat Lao* of the growth of the party from 1951 to 1955. It points out that after the establishment of the Lao Dong party in 1951, the Vietnamese Communists encouraged certain Lao to organize a Communist party in Laos. Guided by Vietnamese advisers, some PL leaders began to develop cells in their zone of operations, resulting in the emergence of party factions in various regions of Laos, each with a different name.[10] Following the Geneva Conference of 1954 when, with the conclusion of the military struggle, the Vietnamese could devote more attention to political organization within Laos, Vietnamese advisers urged the Lao members of the Lao Dong party to organize the various Lao political parties into a single party.[11] This effort resulted in the formation on March 22, 1955, of the PPL.[12]

According to a North Vietnamese economic cadre's notebook, the party soon fell into a dangerous situation when, in 1957 and 1958, a large number of party members were captured and imprisoned or killed. This undoubtedly refers to the period during which integration of the Pathet Lao into the RLG was attempted. In the fall of 1957, Souvanna Phouma and his half-brother Souphanouvong had reached a plan for national reconciliation according to which Souphanouvong and Phoumi Vongvichit would be brought into the government as ministers, the NLHS, or Lao Patriotic Front, would contest the partial elections for the National Assembly scheduled for 1958, the two Pathet Lao-controlled provinces of Sam Neua and Phong Saly would be absorbed into the national government with the NLHS sharing in the appointment of its administrative chiefs, and 1,500 PL soldiers (about one fourth of their total number) would be integrated into the Royal Army in two battalions. Right-wing RLG leaders were dismayed when, during the election in May 1958, the NLHS won nine seats and their allies, the Santiphab party, won four seats, of the total of twenty-one seats contested. These RLG authorities inflicted police surveillance and other harassment upon the newly elected NLHS deputies and their cadres. Following the collapse of negotiations to integrate the two PL battalions into the Royal Army, the Phoui Sananikone government arrested sixteen NLHS leaders, including seven who had been elected to the National Assembly. These leaders were held in prison in Vientiane for approximately a year; they escaped and fled to the

PL-controlled area in May 1960. This neutralization of the top NLHS leadership, most of them presumably PPL leaders, must have been a blow, if only temporary, to the PPL organizational efforts.[13]

Continuing its chronological assessment of the PPL development, the North Vietnamese cadre's notebook points out that in May 1959 the Lao Dong party reestablished a close relationship with the PPL and provided the latter with increased assistance to consolidate the revolutionary movement in Laos. The date for the step-up of Lao Dong assistance to the PPL coincides with the plenum of the Central Committee of the Lao Dong party, held in May 1959, at which Hanoi decided to increase its contribution to the insurgency in South Vietnam. This period marked the beginning of an active North Vietnamese military phase in Laos in which the Communist forces reoccupied Sam Neua and Phong Saly, where an RLG presence had been established after the integration agreements. In the succeeding three years, during the political turbulence within the RLG, Communist forces further advanced to occupy more than half the land area of Laos.[14] The North Vietnamese notebook provides added evidence that the active NVA military phase was accompanied by a concerted North Vietnamese effort to improve the PPL. According to the lessons in the North Vietnamese notebook, the party has steadily improved since the increase in Lao Dong assistance beginning in May 1959.

Semisecrecy of the Party

A distinctive feature of the People's Party of Laos is its semisecret nature.[b] Party members are distributed throughout the major instruments of the NLHS system, principally the army and the bureaucracy. Secret meetings of the party are held, and members are enjoined not to disclose their party affiliation. Nevertheless, from the earliest days of the party, those who are not party members have suspected who the party members were in their units. Several interviewees (A-16, A-18, A-20, A-21, B-9) told us, for example, that they could always guess the members when certain individuals of their military unit were called out to the forest for a clandestine meeting. A number of factors help explain the clandestine nature of the PPL. As one former PL medic (A-10) told us, the party may maintain secrecy because of weakness. Especially in the early years when it was small and could exercise only limited control, the party could give the impression of greater strength than it actually had by shrouding its activity in secrecy—an air of mystery helps create an aura of power. One young former PL officer (A-31) reported that members of his unit were told, "there are many eyes of the Party in all units that see what you do." This warning made the men more vigilant, he contended. By confusing their adversaries, this secrecy may have

---

[b]It appears that some Communist parties in Africa south of the Sahara follow a similar semisecret procedure.

offered a political advantage in negotiations with the RLG, at least in the minds of the PL leaders. Also, during their participation in the Vientiane government they may have found it useful to have a network of party members who were unknown to the opposing factions.

Another reason for the PPL to maintain semisecrecy may have been its desire to create the impression among the Lao population that the NLHS, or Lao Patriotic Front, is not identified with any Communist organization. The PPL strategy called for a reconstitution of a coalition government that reflects the "current realities" of political forces in Laos. The Lao Communist leaders apparently believed that they would lose favor among the Lao population if they avowed that their leading organ is a Communist party. The Lao population, they must have judged, is not yet at the stage of readiness for an open Communist party. This procedure follows Vietnamese Communist practice. During their fighting days the Viet Minh, and now the National Liberation Front (NLF) and the "Alliance," operated with a tightly organized and disciplined clandestine party whose membership, leadership, and power were concealed from the public. Yet, as in the case of Laos, party members were generally known within army ranks, and of course the party wielded the power. The clandestine role of the party which has been transmitted to Laos by the North Vietnamese follows a long historical tradition in Vietnam, as in China, of secret societies.[15]

This semisecrecy has been maintained on the international as well as the internal scene for some of the same reasons. If the PPL is to camouflage its Communist leadership from the Lao public, it would be unwise to advertise itself internationally. Moreover, there is some international diplomatic advantage to be gained, especially in the Third World, for the NLHS to appear as the leader of a nonaligned, national liberation movement, struggling against American imperialism. However, in 1966, a letter of greetings sent by the secretary-general of the PPL Central Committee, Kaysone Phomvihan, was published in the Japanese Communist party's monthly, and a number of similar references to the PPL have subsequently appeared in Communist organs in other parts of the world.[16] In October 1970, the Pathet Lao News Agency broadcasted a long article concerning the Lao liberation struggle by Kaysone. Although he did not use the term People's Party of Laos, Kaysone obviously referred to it when he discussed its origins and development as a "genuine revolutionary party" and clearly distinguished it from the NLHS front.[17]

We can only speculate about the reasons for these relatively scarce references to the PPL in the Communist media abroad. While messages from the Lao Patriotic Front, generally signed by Prince Souphanouvong, appear abundantly in the Soviet and Communist Chinese media, we have found no references to the PPL in their organs. Presumably, the Soviet and Chinese officials who receive PPL messages are familiar with the semisecret position of the PPL and carefully follow an established protocol of discretion. It is possible that the personnel on the Japanese and various East European organs that have published references to the PPL lack familiarity with its semisecret position. As for the DRV reference to the PPL in 1967, it was perhaps the result of an indiscretion. It seems clear that PPL messages are published at the initiation of the receiving party, not the PPL's. The possibility cannot be excluded, however, that as the party grows in strength it does not feel constrained to camouflage its presence among brother parties. Moreover, PPL leaders may wish the status in the socialist world they would achieve following public acknowledgment of their dominant role in the PL region of Laos.[18]

This semisecrecy is one major reason that so little has been known about the People's Party of Laos in the world outside of the Pathet Lao zone. As far as we know, no study of the PPL has previously been published in any language. None of the numerous Soviet and Chinese sources concerned with Laos which we have consulted make reference to the existence of the PPL. Few Lao whom we interviewed, including those who were otherwise familiar with PL practices, had any knowledge of the party. The silence of the PL media during late 1968 and early 1969 about Kaysone, secretary-general of the PPL and presumably the most powerful leader in the Lao Communist organization, provides an example of the party's clandestine style, which makes it difficult for the outsider to understand PPL behavior.[c] There were rumors of his death, yet neither was he reported in attendance at important meetings, as was customary, nor were there other news reports to show he was alive.

Party Revolutionary Doctrine

In view of the close relationship of the People's Party of Laos to the Lao Dong party of the DRV, it is not surprising that the PPL draws heavily upon the revolutionary doctrine of its mentor. Indeed, our evidence shows that Vietnamese advisers frequently prepare the ideological statements used in PPL training sessions. As a comparative basis for our discussion of PPL doctrine, it will be useful to first summarize some of the Lao Dong concepts.[19]

Elements of North Vietnamese Doctrine

North Vietnamese revolutionary doctrine, following the essence of Leninism, places primary importance upon the development of a party to serve as the vanguard of the revolution. Ho Chi Minh's views on the importance of the party are revealed in an observation made by Ho, as recounted by the Vietnamese

---

[c]It is not impossible that during this period Kaysone was in temporary eclipse and there was a factional dispute for power; however, we have no evidence of it. It is possible that Kaystone was wounded or ill and that the PL leadership was reluctant to reveal this information both to their own cadres, whose morale might be shaken by the threatened loss of a leader, and to their enemies, who might exploit their possible loss with propaganda.

Communist leader Truong Chinh, when a young Vietnamese revolutionary in exile in China, prior to the founding of the Indochinese Communist party in 1930, threw a bomb at the car of a French governor-general of Indochina, then on a visit to Canton. Ho was reported to have said that "assassinating Governor-Generals was not the way to achieve the overthrow of the colonial regime. To secure victory for the revolution, a powerful political party was needed."[20]

The founding of the ICP in 1930, according to the DRV official party history, "was not accidental, but was determined by the historical conditions of Vietnam." When the French invaded Vietnam in 1858, the Vietnamese feudal landlord class surrendered to them, opening an epoch in which French monopolists exploited Vietnam, imposing heavy taxes, impoverishing the peasants, and creating a market of cheap labor. Economically, Vietnam, Cambodia, and Laos were turned into private French markets, and politically, a policy of divide and rule was pursued, with the administrative, military, and technical machinery concentrated in French hands. In summary, Vietnam was turned into a market and source of supply of raw materials for the "mother country," and Vietnamese feudal society was transformed into a colonial and semifeudal society. This transformation produced changes in class relationships, which were important to the inevitable revolution. The authoritative DRV study describes the emergence of five principal classes, and shows the role of each in the revolution:[d]

The Vietnamese Feudal Landlord Class. This class, "working hand in glove with the imperialists to maintain its selfish interest," was the object of the revolution. Nevertheless, since the spearhead of the revolution was directed at the "oppressive and aggressive imperialists," a small segment of this class joined the struggle—most of them small landlords, intellectuals, and students of landlord stock.

The Vietnamese Bourgeoisie. Emerging after World War I as Vietnam became both a colonial and semifeudal society, the bourgeoisie split into two parts:

The Comprador-Bourgeoisie. This part included big capitalists who worked as the imperialist agents, buying local products and selling manufactured goods, investing money in industrial and commercial enterprises, and building projects for them. Like the feudal landlord class, this class was an antirevolutionary force.

The National Bourgeoisie. This relatively small group of middle-size capitalists with limited economic power was unable to withstand imperialist competition

---

[d]Although this DRV study does not acknowledge it, this class analysis follows Mao Tse-tung's essay, "On the New Democracy."

and found its interests in contradiction to those of the imperialists and feudalists. At the same time, they had economic relations with them, selling goods, serving as landlords, and thereby exploiting the working class. Thus, the national bourgeoisie had a two-sided nature: on one hand they were against the imperialists and feudalists, favoring national independence and democratic freedom; on the other hand, their attitude was unstable, wavering and hesitant. When the imperialists were strong, the national bourgeoisie compromised and advocated reforms: when the revolutionary mass movement made advances, they tended to support it. Therefore, the national bourgeoisie could not lead the Vietnamese revolution.

The Vietnamese Peasantry. The peasantry, constituting almost 90 percent of the population, was heavily oppressed, having to submit to heavy taxes, high land rent and interest, and corvées. "Short of land, the peasants, first of all the poor and landless peasants, very energetically opposed the imperialists and the feudalists." Therefore, the peasants were the largest revolutionary force and the "most reliable ally of the working class."

Vietnamese Petty Bourgeoisie. Included in this class were craftsmen, traders, owners of small industries, civil servants, intellectuals, and students. While their living standards often differed, they shared a life of instability and threat of unemployment. While they sometimes wavered with the ups and downs of the revolutionary movement, they generally were an important force for the revolution and a reliable ally of the working class.

The Vietnamese Working Class. Emerging with the development of French capitalism in Vietnam after World War I, these workers were the "most revolutionary force, whose political consciousness, organizational ability, discipline and creativeness were higher than those of other classes." Exploited by the imperialists, the feudalists, and the national bourgeoisie, in order to liberate itself the working class had to fight for the emancipation of the whole nation. Its blood ties with the peasantry provided it with favorable conditions to create a worker-peasant alliance. Therefore, though small in number, the Vietnamese working class soon became the leading force of the revolution.

PPL Revolutionary Doctrine

For the analysis that follows, we have drawn upon party training documents, speeches by party leaders, and testimony from several party members. However, our information, although it fills gaps on a subject that has not been studied in any systematic fashion, is still incomplete. One reason for the lack of data is of course the secrecy of the party. Another is the fact that the Lao Communist movement is not so dedicated to keeping records as are the Vietnamese, who fill reams of paper at almost every echelon of organization. In Laos, the rate of literacy is low and the level of education even among those who can read and write is modest. Therefore, the few records one does find are rudimentary. Moreover, the conditions created by continuous fighting and U.S. bombing of the Communist zone made unlikely the development of a body of historical and doctrinal literature.

The analysis is a description of the party revolutionary doctrine, not an evaluation of the party's success in executing it. It must be emphasized that profession of revolutionary premises must not be mistaken for performance. Words are not deeds. In all party programs there is a gap between intentions and realization. In Laos, there are many reasons why there is likely to be an even wider gap between the two than in other Communist systems. The revolutionary doctrine is largely imported and in many respects it has difficulty taking root in Lao soil. Lao culture has not appeared to nurture the competence in disciplined political organizational capability that is called for in this doctrine. In addition, as has been stated before but can hardly be stressed enough, the PL region is undeveloped and impoverished; regional differences are enormous; communication is poor; and the levels of education and technical competence are low. Therefore, the doctrine is not easy to teach or learn. While we do not judge the success in application of the doctrine, we believe it is important as the theoretical underpinning for the Lao Communist leadership. These are some of the concepts the Lao revolutionaries are guided by in their political and military struggle in Laos.

As in the Vietnamese case, the People's Party of Laos adheres to the Leninist doctrine that the existence of a disciplined, genuinely revolutionary party is the key to the revolution. One party document (LP-24) points out that there were earlier heroes in the struggle against the French oppression—Ong Keo, Kommadam, Chao-Fa Patchai, and Pho Kadout[21]—"but they were defeated because there was no Party to lead the struggle." Since the revolution is so complex and difficult, a strong organization is essential and it must win popular support; the document continues: "It may take only pieces of wood to build a fence, but it takes the helping hands of men to build a house." (LP-24)

Following the pattern of Communist parties elsewhere, the PPL recognizes that the key to building an effective party organization is the development of competent, dedicated cadres. Training documents reveal that party members are told they are the vanguard of the revolution. They have gained political consciousness of the contradictions in Lao society and have learned that the only way to free Laos from oppression is through armed struggle. Therefore, they must devote their lives to fulfilling party objectives. Members are admonished that they must not expect personal benefit—promotions or pay—by their party membership. Rather, they join the party to serve the people. One document (LP-9), cataloging the qualities necessary for a party member, describes him as one who is loyal to the nation and willing to serve the people, obeys his leaders without question, keeps good discipline, respects the system, and improves himself through study. Another (LP-24) states that members must be resolute, brave, and undiscouraged in the face of difficulties.

There are certain elements of party procedure, characteristic of Communist parties generally, which the PPL embraces. Party documents proclaim that the party operates upon the principles of democratic centralism with each echelon electing officers in accordance with the "principles of democracy, even if in some cases committee members are appointed by higher echelons as a solution to some special problem." Party affairs are discussed democratically at each echelon and, when a decision is made, the minority must be bound by the majority, individuals must respect group decisions, and lower echelons must submit to the discipline of the higher ones. Criticism and self-criticism are the principal mechanisms for enforcing proper behavior and maintaining coherence in the ideology. Party discipline is strongly inculcated. Discussing party secrecy, one training document (LP-24) points out that the PPL is "obliged to hide in the NLHS [front], even though it acts as the leader of the revolution." The front cannot be the leader since it is "merely an organization of people of various classes . . . not composed of people who are decisive and persistent in their struggle . . . and does not represent the proletariat . . . but rather aims at promoting harmony of all elements."

Marxism-Leninism is proclaimed to be the guiding philosophy of the party. "The resounding victories of the Indochinese peoples in the past quarter century cannot be separated from the introduction of Marxism-Leninism into Indochina," Secretary-General Kaysone stated in late 1970.[22] As one training document (LP-24) puts it, Marxism-Leninism "provides guidance for its action and points out practical ways to advance the revolution in Laos." Although we have not found any sophisticated elaboration of Marxism-Leninism among PL documents—considering the background of the PPL leadership and the nature of the country, it is doubtful that one exists in Laos—we have found the philosophy discussed in several pamphlets. One such pamphlet (EMB-AP13)[23] published in 1963, gives a history of world communism in a simplified form, adapted for a Lao audience. Its preface points out that Marx and Engels discovered the universal principles of communism a century ago, and these have now been embraced by one eighth of the world's population living on one fourth of the earth's surface. "A Communist system," the preface notes, "is gaining ground in our Lao nation. Those classes which abuse power tremble before the Party and its ideology, and attempt to discredit it. But its advance will not be hindered." In a burst of poetic allusion, the preface continues:

Communism is like sunlight at sunrise, chasing the shadows, awakening the workers with its red rays, galvanizing their courage and inciting them to struggle for liberation from oppression.

As does the Vietnamese doctrine, the PPL doctrine defines twin enemies of the Lao people—imperialism and feudalism. The revolution must therefore be a "national *and* a democratic" one. However, the struggle must be carried out "step by step," with the first priority being defeat of the American imperialists. All but a few strata of Lao society must be enlisted in the struggle. "Lackeys" of the American imperialists are constantly denounced as enemies, but "feudalists" are less frequently targeted. At this stage, the party's task is to unite the Lao people in a "broad national united front" to conduct the national liberation war against a foreign enemy and its collaborators.

The PPL follows the broad outline of the Vietnamese class analysis, although class definitions are modified to suit Lao circumstances. (Pathet Lao documents available to us and interviews do not develop this analysis in sufficient detail for our discussion to deal with subtleties. Further investigation might reveal different labels for the class categories. We feel confident, however, that the general thrust of the description is accurate.)

A former PPL member recalled five basic categories of Lao society which he learned in his political lessons:

Upper Bourgeoisie: The king, the royal family, and senior RLG officials, especially those with business interests (this is the first time we have seen the king mentioned in what is designated as an "enemy" category).

National Bourgeoisie: Employers of more than three people, up to and including owners of large enterprises.

Peasants:
Middle Class: own land and produce some surplus rice; work their land, but occasionally hire labor.

Lower Class: own land but do not harvest enough rice to meet their needs; do other work after the harvest season; own land but not draft animals; own draft animals but not land.

Poor farmers: own neither land nor draft animals; hire themselves out to others on a daily wage; catch and sell fish or small game or collect wild vegetables and fruit in jungle.

Petty Bourgeoisie: Small shop owners, school teachers, doctors, farmers who harvest more than 600 kilograms of rice per year but who do not work their land, farmers who own a rice mill, and other farmers who hire labor.

Working Class: Employees in factories and mills, coolies, and itinerant workers on daily or hourly wage.[24]

Although the national and democratic revolution is stated to be in essence "a revolution to liberate the peasantry,"[25] as in the Vietnamese Communist,

Chinese Communist, and Soviet models, the proletariat (working class) is considered the leading force of the revolution. The PPL, according to one training document (LP-24), is the "party of the proletariat," even though it is difficult to find application for this term in Lao reality. This document seems to muddle workers with peasants, describing the proletariat as those who have no land, cattle, or tools for farming, as well as those who sell their labor to factories and workshops. Having undergone the most oppression, they "have been shaped by their experiences in the working class"; they have learned organization and discipline and are therefore the class most fit to lead.

Although PPL training documents pay homage to the Communist thesis that the "solid base Party is the working class," they also recognize, like DRV doctrine, that at the present stage of development in Laos peasants predominate, making up more than 90 percent of the population. Therefore, the worker-peasant alliance of the most oppressed classes constitutes the central core of the party. However, the party must arouse the peasants because many are apathetic about politics.

One document (SAV-12) quotes from prominent international Communist leaders to justify the PPL reliance upon the peasantry as the base of its revolution. Mao Tse-tung is quoted as saying, on the importance of the peasantry to the revolution, "apart from the proletariat, which is the base of the revolutionary Party, the peasants are the largest revolutionary segment of all classes." Ho Chi Minh is quoted: "The peasants are by far the most powerful force of the people; they are loyal friends of the working class; they have great love of country, and great courage for struggle and sacrifice—it is necessary to rely upon the peasants." Finally, Stalin is quoted as saying that the "peasants represent a fundamental force in a national movement—it cannot be otherwise." Thus, the document concludes, the Lao peasants have become, with sacrifice and courage, the true force of the revolution.

The party relies upon the worker-peasant alliance as the base of the revolution; nevertheless it must draw upon other segments of the people. One document entitled *Ten Chapters of Basic Politics* (LP-9) states that all "patriotic Lao" must be mobilized, including students, governmental functionaries, monks, intellectuals, and the national bourgeoisie. The "Lao people," the document states, does not include those "stubborn reactionaries who support the U.S. imperialists, even if they have Lao blood in their veins."

The national bourgeoisie appear to be dealt with along lines similar to those of the Vietnamese model. According to a PPL document, (SAV-12)[26] the national bourgeoisie will watch the progress of the revolution carried out by the worker-peasant alliance. If the revolution seems to be faltering, only a minority of this class will join; however, if it appears on the road to victory, most will support it. Therefore, the party must work out an effective strategy to enlist the national bourgeoisie in the revolution. This strategy must avoid certain mistakes, which are discussed in Leninist dialectics. To ignore differences with the national bourgeoisie, the document contends, would be to abandon the class struggle and to neglect the interests of the working class—an error of the right. Conversely, an unbridled attack against the national bourgeoisie, driving them from the revolution, would be an error of the left. This strategy of mobilizing all "patriotic Lao" into a temporary alliance is the party's front policy, carried out under the aegis of the NLHS, which we shall discuss in the next chapter.

The doctrine denounces feudalism, yet there is no Lao equivalent of the Vietnamese landlord class. Laos does not have a major problem of land alienation, as did Vietnam or China in prerevolutionary days. Land is relatively abundant, there is little land pressure, and, to judge by the silence on this subject in party documents, great landlords are not defined as a principal enemy. As we shall show below, land reform does not appear as a theme in the NLHS platform. When Anna Louise Strong interviewed the NLHS woman deputy Madame Khampheng Boupha in the early 1960s, she was told that "land reform was no problem, because Laos has a surplus of land." Prince Souphanouvong in another interview with Miss Strong confirmed this statement.[27]

The People's Party of Laos recognizes that the conduct of the revolution must conform to the conditions in Laos and need not be identical with the pattern in other Communist countries. A former party member stated that he was told that, whereas Russia as a more developed country could base its revolution upon the workers, Laos would have to rely upon the peasants. Further, he learned that, following consolidation of Communist Chinese power in 1949, land was confiscated, but in Laos, where there are few large land owners, such policies need not apply. One party document (SAV-12) describes the revolutions in Russia, Vietnam, China, and Cuba as having used a joint political and military struggle, but in the Lao revolution it was necessary first to use arms and only afterwards "for better or worse, undertake the political struggle."

Elaborating on the party's strategy and tactics in a speech in October 1970, Secretary-General of the Party Kaysone declared:

The party has mobilized the masses to wage a struggle in many forms closely combining armed struggle with political struggle, making use of various forms of struggle—legal, diplomatic, parliamentary, several negotiations, two national coalition governments . . . but the party always regards armed struggle and political struggle as the two fundamental ones, the former being the most important form to win victory.

Elaborating further on the Pathet Lao revolutionary doctrine, Kaysone stated:

The Lao revolution shows that in a small country with a backward economy and culture and a nascent working class like Laos which has to cope with imperialism having powerful economic and military potential . . . if one can build a revolutionary party with a thorough revolutionary spirit, a correct military and political line . . . a close-knit organization, an inner unity, firm ties with the masses, and total dedication to the people, which knows how to mobilize and organize the masses for the struggle, promote the tradition of resistance against foreign invasion and enlist the assistance of fraternal countries, in the first place the socialist countries, then the revolution, though beset with difficulties and hardships, will certainly triumph.[28]

Function of the Party

The People's Party of Laos, like Communist parties in all countries where they have seized power, defines its role as "the supreme directing organization in all domains," (LP-24) and generally follows the pattern of ruling Communist parties elsewhere. Listing the several favorable factors for the national liberation struggle in Laos, Kaysone concludes that "the fundamental and determining factor remains the correct leadership of the genuine party."[29]

One authority on Communist organization points out that in the Soviet and Chinese party concept the party has no specific concrete task as a ministry has, but rather is "an organization in which leaders are gathered in a context which strengthens their capacity to lead." The party develops moral-political leadership that is exercised in some other organizational role, not in the party itself. "Party members go forth from Party meetings armed with new policy instructions from the leadership and activated by new ideological and political indoctrination."[30] In this pattern, PPL cadres are distributed throughout the principal institutions in the PL system, particularly the army, the front, and the administration, where they are expected to provide dedicated, selfless leadership. The PPL achievement in placing competent cadres in its key organizations is far from the Soviet, Chinese, or North Vietnamese models, as one would expect in the Lao context, an issue we shall discuss below.

A North Vietnamese adviser (B-9) to a Pathet Lao battalion, Captain Mai Dai Hap, described the role of PPL members where he was assigned:

The mission of the party is to command and direct—in any activity, combat, discipline, organization—everything. For example, before an offensive, the party members meet together to discuss the offensive. Then, they get together with the rest of the men in the battalion, and provide them guidance.

Extending his remarks to describe the role of the party in the administration of PL Nam Tha Province, Hap said:

The function of the party is the same as I described it in the army. The party command controls everything. In each separate functional branch of the province administrative committee, whether it be propaganda, economic affairs, the front, whatever, there are cells of party members who get together to develop a policy for their particular branch. Of course, in my province, though they had the intention of directing things, they did a poor job.[31]

Party members are constantly exhorted that their behavior must set an example for the rest of the population to achieve the revolutionary tasks. In addressing a convocation of party members from Xieng Khouang Province, a party secretary set out the tasks facing the membership. (We select only some principal ideas to provide a sample of his major points.)

1. Patiently endure all hardships and difficulties. Strengthen the determination to fight against the American imperialists and their lackeys. . . .
2. Develop correct ideologies for people of different classes and ethnic groups.
3. Improve the political life of the Party. Maintain strict discipline within the Party . . . augment the prestige of the Party, and lead others to adhere to its policies and instructions.
4. Strengthen the regular armed forces, the paramilitary forces, and the militia and the guerrillas in the provinces and districts.
5. Cement harmony among members of the Party and people of various ethnic groups. . . .[32]

Selection of Members

Our evidence makes it clear that the most ambitious, zealous, and able individuals are invited to apply for membership in the People's Party of Laos. Criteria for admission to the PPL provided by one source include: a good political background; enthusiasm in the performance of tasks; trust by the people; and voluntary application for party membership. An obvious disqualifier for membership is "any relation with the enemy." A candidate member of the party, who claimed that his upper-class family background hindered his admission, described the criteria for membership in the PPL. Prospective members must show qualities of leadership, excellence of performance at their assignments, readiness to submit to party discipline, and willingness to commit themselves fully to the goals of the revolution. Favor is shown to those in the lower socioeconomic classes, largely peasants or workers, though the party is open to those considered "capable of thinking like a member of the lower classes."

A former PL district chief (chau muong) (A-16) whom we interviewed said that he had served in administrative posts for almost ten years but was not invited to join the party because he was the son of a canton chief (tasseng):

They believed that the offspring of the ruling class had developed habits of capitalists. They charged that these people were not sound or determined—they are easily carried along by anybody. So they didn't trust me.

Asked what he believed to the PPL criteria for membership, he replied:

Only the poor who were hard workers and had experienced oppression by the ruling class, such as those with relatives who had been killed, or those who had oppressed by capitalists, or who were haunted with hatred against them.[33]

In fact, most of the leading party figures do not meet the criterion of lower-class social origin. However, it is not uncommon, as the Vietnamese experience suggests, for members of the bourgeoisie to join Communist-led nationalist movements during the period of agitation for independence.[34] After the achievement of independence, and as the Communist party consolidates power, more stringent Marxist-Leninist class criteria for Party membership are imposed, which is apparently also the case in Laos.

Candidates for membership may be proposed by any full member. First, the cell or group to which he is proposed must give its unanimous approval, and approval from the next higher echelon must be secured. The candidate is observed for some three months before he is invited to submit a written application for membership.

We have examined an application for membership in which the applicant expressed his fervent intent:

To fight throughout my life for the benefit of the Party, the nation, and the revolution, from the beginning to the end; to regard the work for the common good as my primary task and to sacrifice unconditionally my own interests to the interests of the Party, the nation, and the revolution; to lead the revolution to the final goal, to liberate the people of my own class to make the nation completely independent; to observe strictly all orders; and to absolutely maintain Party secrets. Even if I am captured and tortured by the enemy, I will never reveal Party secrets.

The applicant submitted a biography showing his family background, education, occupation, ethnic identity (lowland Lao), class (poor), religion (Buddhist), technical knowledge ("I know how to operate a sewing machine"), social habits ("I never play cards and never raped a girl"), and politics ("I never made contact with the enemy"). Following his biography, the applicant stated his weak points ("I do not have any experience in military tactics") and his strong points, which showed how diligently he had worked as a Lao Patriotic Front cadre.

The period of probation extends from six months for candidates from the lower classes to nine months for those of the middle class, and up to three years for certain members of royalty or wealthy families (though, according to our source, this period could be shortened by the party hierarchy). During the trial period, the candidate receives political training and must participate in self-criticism sessions regularly. When finally approved for admission, the candidate is admitted to full membership at an initiation ceremony.

The leadership of the Pathet Lao movement, as we have pointed out, has been dominated from the outset by lowland Lao. At least since 1962, perhaps earlier, the PPL leadership has made a special effort to increase its membership among the highland minorities. Directing this effort within the organization and membership staff of the PPL are three separate sections: one for Lao Soung affairs (Meo, Yao), another for Lao Theung affairs, and a third for Lao Loum affairs. Certain exceptions to party regulations were made for ethnic minorities, such as relaxation of the prohibition of marriage before the age of thirty. In addition, the PPL made a special effort to see that the minority party members could obtain their native food and clothing, even if this might create some hardship among the majority Lao membership. In response to complaints by minority leaders about lack of opportunity for their children to study abroad, preference was reportedly given for scholarships to the children of minority candidates for study in the Soviet Union, Communist China, and other Communist countries.

A notation in the aforementioned North Vietnamese cadre's notebook, apparently referring to late 1967 when these political figures were recorded, gives the following ethnic breakdown for party members: Lao Theung, 60.02 percent; Lao Loum, 36.7 percent; and Lao Soung, 3.08 percent. These figures, if accurate, would demonstrate that PPL leaders assign importance to building their party base among the ethnic minorities. Since the PL zone is populated by only 20 percent lowland Lao, these statistics are credible. Such a party composition would suggest that in the future, when the new party recruits gain seniority, there will be greater representation of ethnic minorities in the top PPL leadership now dominated by lowland Lao.

Training

Training is an important part of the formation of a reliable party cadre. Members and candidate members are given special training and self-criticism sessions. Higher-level cadres generally instruct lower-level cadres, though there is also a certain amount of instruction among members of the same group.

A frequently used method is for the teacher to dictate a series of questions, followed by their answers. Much of the literature we gathered in the field consists of such question-and-answer materials. For example, one training document that has turned up in various Pathet Lao areas of Laos contains twelve basic questions and answers about the party. These questions include: Why do we say that our party alone will lead the people to a successful revolution? What is the objective of the struggle of our party? What is the doctrine of our party? Our discussion above of party doctrine provides an insight into the answers that members are expected to learn, if not memorize. Members, even of equal rank, can pose these questions to each other and check the answers from their notebooks. The method clearly stresses the inculcation of a set of party principles and the formation of a reliable "revolutionary" frame of mind.

An important segment of the training sessions is devoted to internal party matters, such as the instruction for organizing effective party units at each echelon. Some sessions deal with the fulfillment of particular tasks, such as the measures for consolidating a newly "liberated" area. Other lessons are addressed to special problems. For example, a PPL document written in 1967, found in

Xieng Khouang Province, was devoted to "countering the psychological warfare of the enemy," explaining what party members should do to deal with propaganda aimed at the local population. Simple political lessons are often contained in the the training documents, with instructions that party members teach these lessons to the people.[35]

A graduate of the Kommadam Officers School who attended from January 1 to April 1, 1963, with 300 other students, reported that he and others received a special seven-day course devoted exclusively to a study of the history, regulations, and organization of the People's Party of Laos. Because of the party's semisecrecy, it is not clear whether all students or only specially selected ones were present at these sessions. Khamtay Siphandone, supreme commander of the Lao People's Liberation Army, gave the opening lecture devoted to the history of the party; its organization, rules, and regulations; and Marxism-Leninism. Following his lecture, the students were divided into groups of six or seven, from each of which the best qualified person was selected as group leader. For each subsequent morning and afternoon session, the group leader would pick up a list of questions based on some aspect of Khamtay's lecture. As a few political instructors passed from group to group to monitor the performance, these questions would be posed to each member of the small group until it was clear that all had learned the answers. On the final day of instruction, Khamtay gave a lecture to the entire class, and books were distributed to each student upon graduation.[36]

Discipline, Rewards, and Punishment

Like most Communist parties in their early stages, the PPL places great emphasis upon proper "revolutionary" behavior. Although to the outsider the exhortations in the PPL training documents appear as platitudinous demands for virtue, they seem concrete to the indoctrinated. The former candidate member of the PPL whom we quoted above reviewed some of the more important regulations for members:

Be honest in party matters . . . defend the party against all threats . . . do not betray the confidence of the people . . . place party interests above personal ones . . . keep party secrets at all cost . . . be faithful to the party . . . do not cause internal party strife . . . work constantly for self-improvement . . . set a good example for the common people. . . .

Frequent self-criticism meetings are scheduled to review the behavior of party members. Party leaders at every echelon are reminded to praise publicly those cadres who perform well, and although those who do not live up to party standards must be admonished, they must be helped, too. Though many of our interviewees complained of boredom at the frequent criticism sessions, they also admitted that these sessions were a useful device in guiding behavior.

The party dispenses a series of formal awards to outstanding members. The First Victory Medal is the highest award, followed by the Second and Third Victory Medals. Special letters of commendation are sent by the Secretary-General Kaysone to specially deserving party members. Heroism in battle for party members in the military is recognized by the Lenin award.

Party members are expected to make certain personal sacrifices. Communist puritanism has been introduced, which clashes with the natural Lao gaiety and love for the pleasures of life. Party members are to discourage the people's inclination for frequent festivals ("bouns"), celebrations, lavish marriages, and funerals. Party members should not drink or gamble, nor dally with the girls—delights a young Lao does not easily shun. As pointed out above, lowland Lao party members are prohibited from marrying before the age of thirty, a hardship for many.

A party member may be accused of misbehavior by any other member. In such a case, investigation is made by his immediate party organization and a vote is taken to levy the proper punishment, which may include suspension or expulsion from the party. In the event of infractions by higher-level cadres, the Internal Defense Organization makes an investigation.

Size and Organization

In the absence of published figures about its composition, it is not possible to make an authoritative statement about the PPL's size. However, from several sources we have located similar estimates of the party's number. A PPL document dated 1965, captured at Xieng Khouang Ville in April 1969, gave PPL total membership as approximately 12,000. A former PPL member captured in August 1969 estimated that in 1965 PPL had 11,000 members, including probationary and permanent members in military and civilian organizations. The notebook of the North Vietnamese economic cadre mentioned above, apparently referring to early 1968, put party size at 14,000. Using one million as an estimate of the PL zone population and 14,000 as PPL membership, 1.4 percent of the population would be party members. (This compares with 5.77 percent of the Soviet population who were full members of the Communist party in 1969.)

We find constant emphasis in PPL communications, similar to the exhortations in People's Revolutionary party documents in South Vietnam, to expand the ranks of the party.[37] A Xieng Khouang party committee document, dated July 29, 1965, urges enlargement of the party. A document discovered in November 1965 in another PL-controlled area (Nong Khang) points out, however, that although expansion is the most important party activity, a strong party depends not only on quantity but on quality as well. A speech by the

Xieng Khouang party secretary on March 22, 1969, revealed that 1969 was the second year of a three-year plan for the entire PL zone which emphasized expansion of the party as one of three major tasks.[e]

The PPL has at least a skeletal organization in most if not all provinces. That organization is portrayed in Figures 2-1 and 2-2. Following the general

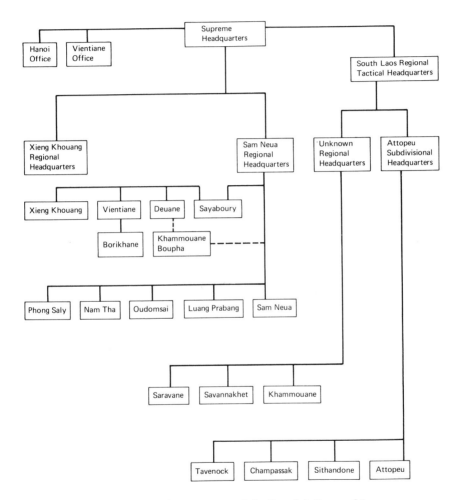

Figure 2-1. The Organization of the People's Party of Laos

[e]The second was the launching of a vigorous dry-season military operations plan, which was achieved; and the third was implementation of certain economic measures such as the distribution of a new PL currency, the "liberation Kip" notes, which was carried out.

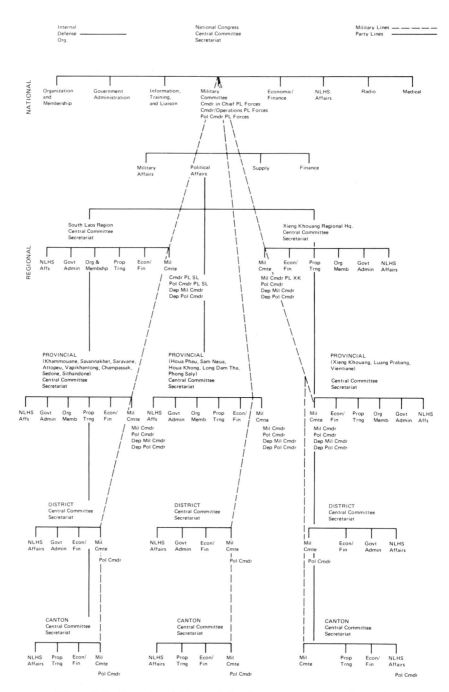

Figure 2-2. Functional Chart of the Organization of the People's Party of Laos

Communist practice, the National Congress, which is supposed to meet annually, is presumed to be the highest governing body of the PPL. In fact, the Central Committee exercises the actual control over the party. Members of the Central Committee are normally selected for a six-year term, by secret ballot of all party members. The first election was held in 1956; the second did not take place until 1964. In September 1968, the Central Committee of the PPL was composed of the following members (only eleven positions, instead of the authorized fifteen, were filled).

Kaysone Phomvihan	Secretary-General
Nouhak Phongsavan	Deputy Secretary-General
Prince Souphanouvong	First Committee Member (and Chairman of NLHS)
Phoumi Vongvichit	Foreign Affairs
Sisomphone	PPL Organization and Membership
Samseun	PPL Internal Security
Sanan	
General Khamtay Siphandone	Supreme Commander, PL Forces
General Sisavat	Chief of Staff
General Saman	Chief of Staff, Political Affairs
Khamsouk	First Secretary, South Laos

In addition to cadres assigned to work for the Central Committee members, the Central Committee has a separate staff organization directed by Sisomphone, which includes organization and membership; governmental administration; information, training and liaison; economic and finance; NLHS affairs; radio broadcasting; and medicine. The military committee staff is further subdivided into military affairs, political affairs, supply, and finance. The PPL has a liaison office in Hanoi, referred to as Office 98.

As Figure 2-2 shows, there is a district headquarters below each province and at the base of the hierarchy is the canton. At each echelon there is a central committee served by a secretariat. The regional and provincial levels of the central committee are served by six sections: NLHS affairs, governmental administration, organization and membership, propaganda and training, economic and finance, and military affairs. At the lower levels there are no special sections for organization and membership or for propaganda and training.

It is clear that this framework of party activity follows the Vietnamese Communist model. It should be repeated that the NLHS, like the National Liberation Front of South Vietnam (NLSVN), is presented to public view as the governing authority, but the party (like the People's Revolutionary party in South Vietnam) exercises the policy-making authority. It is interesting, too, that the military is subordinate to party control at each echelon of the hierarchy although, as the chart shows, the military has its own lines of authority to superior echelons. Emphasis upon political guidance of the military is also evident from the fact that in each military committee there is not only a commander for military affairs but one for political affairs as well (a fuller discussion of the Lao People's Liberation Army (LPLA) organization is in Chapter 4).

The PPL has an Internal Defense Organization whose chief, Samseun, reports only to Kaysone. Membership in this organization is secret; it investigates activities of PPL members, operating as a control device to maintain party probity and discipline.

In recent years the National Congress of the PPL has met in October (at the beginning of the dry season) with an estimated 300 to 400 persons normally in attendance, including a civilian and a military delegation from each province. Generally members of the central committee for each region and province attend the National Congress, with at least one of the members remaining behind to manage party affairs. Because of the danger from air strikes, the general session has been held in a large cave (50 meters long, 30 meters wide, 20 meters high) that served as a party headquarters at other times. The cave has a floor paved with concrete, lights, a public address system provided by its own generator, and the capacity to seat the entire audience.

Sometime prior to the National Congress session, reports are compiled throughout the party organization summarizing the past year's activities. At the general session, each delegation is called upon to report on the successes and failures in its jurisdiction during the year and to listen to the party's plan for the coming year. These reports are presented during the first two or three days of the session, following the opening speech by Kaysone the Party Secretary-General or Nouhak the Deputy Secretary-General. A discussion of these reports is held during the next two to four days, followed by presentation of the party's general report, usually by Kaysone. Khamtay Siphandone, supreme commander of the LPLA, then reports on military affairs. After four days devoted to the reports of Kaysone and Khamtay, a two-week adjournment of the general session normally follows. The delegates are then organized, at random, into groups of approximately 10 persons each for self-criticism sessions and to discuss successes and failures, strengths and weaknesses, during the past year. A leader of each group is then required to report the results to the director of the congress.

Following the self-criticism sessions, the general session reconvenes to listen to the party's general plan for the coming year, to ask questions about it, and to discuss it. After adjournment of the congress, some delegates take vacations, ranging from a week to a month, usually either in Sam Neua or Hanoi. In the past, the Soviet Union has offered fifteen-day paid vacations for fifteen party members and the Chinese Communists have provided one-month vacations for twenty members, all chosen by the party secretary-general or his deputy. The vacationers traveled by car to Hanoi, then by air to either the Soviet Union or

China. Most delegates, it appears, preferred to go to the Soviet Union because it was more modern than China.

A process similar to that conducted at the National Congress is apparently repeated throughout the year at each echelon of the party. A document dated 1965 reveals this and shows instructions to lower echelons on procedures for holding general meetings, electing executive committees, and reviewing party activities. An excerpt with instructions for organizing a party congress reveals the central concerns of the provincial party committee:[f]

Report on the results of the past year's work, such as the building of local guerrilla forces, defending the villages and districts against enemy actions, the building of foundations and administrative organizations of the canton and the village, maintaining of the peace, the increase in production to better the living standard of the people, the improvement of the educational, cultural, and social level, the carrying out of the tribal policy (unification), and the improvement of the Party and its cadres.

The significance of the party cadres in a country as poorly developed as Laos is obvious. It is not surprising, therefore, that PPL Secretary-General Kaysone in the previously cited article of October 1970 referred to the "tested contingent of Party cadres and members" as a major asset of the Lao revolution.[38]

The North Vietnamese and the PPL

We have shown the critical role of the North Vietnamese in the PPL's historical development of the People's Party of Laos. There is recent evidence that Hanoi's support for its growth and improvement continues.[39] The North Vietnamese assign cadres to serve as PPL advisers down through the district (muong) level of the PPL. For example, according to a North Vietnamese document left behind after the Royal Lao Government attack on the Plain of Jars during 1969, five North Vietnamese advisers were assigned to the Xieng Khouang provincial committee and eleven additional political advisers were assigned to the provincial government.[40] But even North Vietnamese cadres whose principal assignment is not with the party but is with, say, military or economic units, are required to devote close attention to developing the PPL cells in their jurisdiction since, as we have pointed out, DRV doctrine assigns top priority to the creation of a strong party.

An entry in the North Vietnamese cadre's notebook suggests that the North Vietnamese assistance program was the subject of a formal Lao Dong

---

[f]It is interesting that this document, which was handwritten in Lao, was also found in typewritten form in the Vietnamese language, suggesting that the guidance for these party orders came from a Vietnamese adviser who dictated, or had translated, these Vietnamese instructions into Lao.

party resolution in 1955, amended on June 10, 1967.[g] Assistance provided by the North Vietnamese advisers runs the gamut of party activities, as revealed by the North Vietnamese's notebook. North Vietnamese cadres in Laos are taught to assist in selecting dynamic and aggressive cadres to strengthen the party organization, the administration, the guerrillas, and the youths' and women's forces. Recruitment should be particularly active among poor farmers and workers "who are constantly oppressed." North Vietnamese cadres must help to set up training programs, especially for those cadres who operate at the village level. They are instructed to give more attention to the development of PPL village chapters—the instructions call for the establishment of "four-knowledge" party chapters whose members should be indoctrinated to improve "their ideological knowledge and fighting spirit, and to eliminate their fear of death and sacrifice, their reliance on superiors, and their love of leisure." (It appears that four-knowledge party chapters are a DRV party organizational campaign technique.) Instructions are provided that more party cells must be organized among village guerrillas. Help must be provided in dealing with routine party business, developing improved staff techniques, and scheduling regular congresses.

Our evidence gives us some insights into North Vietnamese judgments of the PPL's competence. Regarding the quality of PPL members, the cadre's notebook, assessing the period from 1960 to 1967, states that "only 25 percent display a good sense, 30 percent display a fair sense, and 45 percent display too poor a sense of leadership." Further, it notes that "a large number of Party members still display a poor fighting spirit." In fighting two wars, first against the French and now against the Americans, "a large number of Party members have become discouraged." The cause of this discouragement is attributed, in characteristic Vietnamese Communist fashion, to the "weak political awareness" of party members. Further, in commenting upon the weakness in all cadres, party and others, the notebook points out that there are still too few cadres drawn from the exploited classes, the minority groups, youths, and women. Most cadres are too old, lack specialized skills, have little knowledge of economics, and suffer from poor educational and political backgrounds. Commenting upon a PPL policy weakness, the notebook states that military activities have been given precedence, unwisely, over political activities. An organizational shortcoming has been the emphasis placed upon improving party central headquarters while neglecting the creation of local party chapters.

Former Captain Mai Dai Hap (B-9), pointing out the PPL shortcomings from his vantage point as a military adviser to an LPLA battalion from 1964 to 1966, said that party cells in his battalion were not at full strength, when compared with those of the North Vietnamese. Whereas an NVA battalion with a normal complement of 500 men would have a party organization of from 70 to 80 members, the LPLA battalion, he advised, which had 300 to 350 men, had a PPL organization of only 14. An NVA company, with 100 to 120 men, would have

---

[g]Since Lao Dong resolutions are secret, we could find no further information about the resolution or the amendment.

20 to 30 party members; the companies in his battalion, each of 70 to 90 men, had PPL cells of only 3 or 4 each. An NVA platoon with 30 men would have 7 to 10 party members; the platoons in his battalion had only 0 to 3 members each. Evaluating the reasons for this weakness, Hap said,

In the PL they lack propaganda and recruiting cadres for developing new Party members. The higher echelons don't give adequate guidance. The incumbent party officers are not competent—they don't know how to work or to supervise their subordinates. Though there are some courageous soldiers, they don't know anything about how to recruit or to make party propaganda.

It is important to remind ourselves that these are judgments from North Vietnamese sources, drawing their criteria from Lao Dong party practice. Most observers would agree that the North Vietnamese Communists have demonstrated a remarkable talent for political organization and their evaluations are therefore rigorous and perhaps reflect some condescension. Moreover, the criticisms taken from the North Vietnamese cadre's notebook reflect the constant effort by North Vietnamese advisory personnel to improve the weaknesses in their "sister" party, thus providing continuous pressure and guidance for strengthening the PPL.

When judged by Vietnamese Communist standards, it is little wonder that PPL achievements appear deficient. However, by Lao standards the growth and persistence of the PPL represent no small accomplishment. Most of the political parties that were organized on the RLG side over the past two decades dissolved within a few years.

We can only speculate about the fate of the PPL if one day it should no longer continue to receive assistance from DRV advisers. In the PPL's favor, it can be noted that it has grown to an estimated 10,000 to 15,000 members in the past twenty years, and its cadres have gained considerable experience. During this period these cadres have been training in North Vietnam and, to a lesser extent, in China, the Soviet Union, and a few Eastern European countries. There have been no public fissures in the party leadership. On the doubtful side, it must be noted that Lao cultural characteristics do not lend themselves easily to sustained political organization, and without the assistance of competent, committed North Vietnamese advisers the PPL would have difficulties maintaining cohesion and control. The party has not yet gone through a generational change of leadership—its founders are still in power. Other Communist parties have shown great stress at periods of imminent, or actual, leadership succession and the PPL may not be immune to similar conflict. The death of Lenin led to factional struggles between Stalin and Trotsky in the Soviet Union, and in China, as Mao Tse-tung approached his mid-seventies, internal party cleavages were revealed. It would not be surprising, therefore, to find splits emerging within the PPL which could seriously damage the relatively young party.

Concluding Observations

As we suggested at the outset, the creation of a coherent zonewide (if not nationwide) political organization, with a membership and system of authority reaching from a central headquarters to the villages, represents a substantial and unique accomplishment in a country so low on the development scale as is Laos. The organization appears active, growing, and increasingly influential.

A number of factors contribute to making the party a cohesive instrument of rule. The party can reward—in promotion, praise, power, and prestige—those who serve its interests and punish those who do not. Certain rituals and processes induce members to identify with the party. For example, party congresses at all levels frequently bring members together, reminding them that, though they may reflect the great diversity in Laos, they are serving a common institution. Training teaches discipline in following party regulations. Political indoctrination inculcates a sense of a common cause, emphasizing that all cadres exhibit Lao patriotism, regardless of regional, tribal, or ethnic origin. Further, the party maintains that it is leading a national liberation struggle against foreign imperialists, first the French and now the Americans. Thus, the party has introduced an institutionalized political interest to replace fragmented and particularistic ones.

However, although it may have introduced a modicum of unity within the zone it controls, the party has contributed to disunity in the country as a whole. Identified intimately with the Vietnamese Communist party since its origin, the PPL leadership has widened the gap between itself and the non-Communist leadership as the Vietnam war has escalated. The institutionalization of a Communist party leadership in the PL zone accentuates the differences in the two parts of Laos, making integration even more difficult to achieve.

Because of the growing strength of the party in the PL zone, it is important to examine the changes in leadership patterns that are likely to emerge. A new source of future leaders has been tapped by party recruiting techniques. Traditionally, leadership selection in Laos has rested on regional and tribal custom, with emphasis given to age, status in the community and, particularly among the lowland Lao, upper-class origins. By contrast, party recruitment favors youth, lower-class origins, and certain attitudes deemed wholesome for a Communist cadre, such as inclination "to serve the revolution." This gives importance to identification with the party, not the locality. Moreover, party recruitment seems to be vigorous among ethnic minorities, suggesting a much more important role for them in the future. In addition, a new style of behavior is emerging. Certain graceful qualities of the Lao personality are eroded in the well-trained party cadre. The gentleness, desire to avoid conflict, and other-worldliness of the Theravada Buddhist give way to the more rigid, combative revolutionary. Gaiety and self-indulgence are challenged by abstemiousness and hard work. However, Lao traits and habits are not easily rubbed out. The result of indoctrinating a young Lao party candidate is most often not a *Communist* cadre, but a *Lao Communist* cadre.

Of course, judgments about the quality of the PPL cadres are relative. North Vietnamese soldiers and advisers serving in Laos, accustomed to the severity of their own party cadres, tend to view even the well-indoctrinated Lao cadre as somewhat lazy and frivolous. On the other hand, former PL personnel and refugees from PL zones are impressed by the zeal and vigor of the PPL cadres. These informants who have fled the PL system do not find the cadres endearing—far from it. They consider them humorless, rigid, and sanctimonious and find tedious their constant outpouring of Communist slogans. Nevertheless, they show a grudging respect for the cadres' dedication and probity, and they recognize, with regret, the cadres' ability to impose their will.

It is unlikely that the PPL would have reached its present level of development without the inspiration and guidance of the North Vietnamese Communists. Recognizing this crucial Vietnamese role, however, is not to deny that the party has roots in Lao soil and represents an important political adversary to the RLG. Indeed, though the non-Communist leadership have enjoyed significant outside material support, they have not been guided toward, nor have they achieved, the construction of any equivalent modern, nationwide political organization. It is too early to say whether or not the PPL, despite its heavy dependence on Vietnamese guidance, is beginning to reflect the worldwide trend toward diversity and autonomy in the world Communist movement. One might read such a meaning into the previously cited key article by Kaysone of October 1970 in which he refers to the need for the Lao revolutionary party to apply principles (of revolution) "creatively."[41]

3 Politics and Administration

Most of what is Laos today was never under a single ruler except for brief periods. Although cultural and ethnic ties linked the lowland Lao, certain regions were independent principalities. Within each principality local leaders exercised authority with little interference. French rule reinforced this pattern, superimposing a French-directed bureaucracy composed of Vietnamese at the second echelon and Lao generally at the third echelon. However, the colonial administration did not penetrate many areas and the authority structure was not much changed, particularly at the canton and village level. During the French colonial period there was little politicization of the rural dwellers, who remained largely unaware of any outside government or administration.

The Lao Communist authorities, with Vietnamese guidance, have introduced fundamental changes in this familiar pattern. In the areas where they dominate they have brought national politics to the village level and have enlarged the scope of administration and control. Their doctrine, rooted in Vietnamese Communist practice, stresses two political tasks: propaganda (education) and organization. In what they designate, following Communist doctrine, as a "national and democratic revolution" under conditions of "people's war," they seek not simply passive acceptance or obedience from the population but active participation.

Besides being doctrinally committed to the politics of participation the Lao Communists place heavy demands upon the population of their zone. First, they need young men to serve in their military forces. Second, they need resources, meaning taxes, generally in the form of rice or other food. Third, they need work to support their system, generally corvée labor to perform porterage duty, road-building, and similar tasks. To fulfill these requirements, considering their underdevelopment they have erected a rather complicated political and administrative structure, which we shall describe.

Any discussion of the Pathet Lao political and administrative organization must be made, of course, within the context of the environmental and cultural conditions of Laos. We have discussed the regional diversity and ethnic complexity of the country and have alluded to its primitive economic and social condition. There is much truth in the remark that "Laos is more a geographic expression than a nation." In controlling territory that is the more backward and heterogeneous of divided Laos, the Pathet Lao authorities face an even greater challenge than did their Royal Lao Government adversaries.

Since cultural factors are particularly important to politics and administra-

41

tion, it may be worthwhile to comment briefly upon certain characteristics of Laos. Laos has been described as a loosely structured society whose people are tolerant and permissive. Those who travel from Vietnam find the Lao more gay and carefree, giving more time to distraction and laughter than do the Vietnamese. Village festivals ("bouns") and "bacis"—a joyful ceremony to celebrate important family occasions—are frequent. The description of the ethnic minorities of Laos, found in the North Vietnamese cadre's notebook, as "natural, joyful, warm, simple-mannered, and honest" is a familiar one. Traditional Lao social relations in Laos seemed aimed at avoiding conflict, and the typical Lao will shun unpleasant confrontations.

The Lao seem less committed to seeking material achievement than are their Vietnamese neighbors. Their manner is more easy-going, making them appear more inclined to relax than to strive, to coast rather than to drive. They do not display assiduous work habits, which led the French colonial rulers and Vietnamese to regard them as indolent. This view is reflected in the novels of a French writer, Hougron, whose books are set in colonial Indochina. In one, he has a Eurasian (French-Vietnamese) rubber plantation foreman give the following formula of work output for the Indochinese peoples: one Tonkinese = five Annamese = ten Cochinchinese = fifteen Cambodians = twenty-five Lao.

These observations are not meant to demean Lao cultural traits. On the contrary, the Lao show delightful and admirable qualities of warmth, easy hospitality, and friendliness. There seems to be a harmony to life in Laos; strife has been low and tolerance for deviance high. Thus, it has been possible for great diversity to persist without meeting strong demands for conformity.

Laos has not experienced intense economic and social pressures that have contributed, in other Asian countries, to political activism. Aspirations have not outpaced acquisition, as they have in much of the Third World. Sparsely inhabited for its expansive land area, Laos has not had great population pressure. Rural areas were little affected by French presence, and even in the cities the French impact—compared with that of Vietnam—was slight. As a consequence, Lao nationalism did not reach the intensity or fervor of Vietnam's. There was no serious land alienation in Laos. It should be clear that the PL leaders have not responded to widespread mass appeal for liberation or improvement. Rather, in this relatively "soft" political and social environment PL leaders are attempting to inspire a revolutionary commitment.

The PL leaders have set as their ambitious task the creation of a new society. They have slim resources—both human and material—to accomplish this task. Their commitment to the politics of participation is a radical change from traditional practice.

As they build a new society, the PL authorities, guided by Vietnamese mentors, are attempting to alter some of the Lao cultural traits and practices we have described. They discourage as wasteful and expensive the frequent "bouns" and "bacis." Their aim is to replace the easy tolerance of deviant behavior and relaxed attitude toward work with new revolutionary standards of morality and behavior. They are attempting to abolish primitive practices and superstition, such as propitiation of the "phi"—the malevolent and benevolent spirits inhabiting the countryside which influence one's life.

During most of the past quarter of a century the PL have been engaged in an armed struggle. The years since 1964 have been the most onerous, since the PL have been subjected to powerful U.S. air bombardments. Party, front, and government headquarters are located in caves, and leaders as well as followers must adjust to the bombing. In areas subject to frequent attacks, particularly those where PL and North Vietnam troops are located, work in the fields and other tasks are carried out at times of least danger, particularly at dawn and dusk, and people live in caves or dugouts. Some towns—Khang Khay, Xieng Khouang, Phong Savan, to mention a few—have been completely leveled.

These wartime conditions have placed heavy burdens upon the political and administrative systems. While certain factors we have mentioned inhibit revolutionary change, among them the low intensity of nationalism, the absence of land hunger or population pressure, and the low level of "rising expectations," the state-of-siege environment creates conditions favoring radical change. The great mobility caused by the danger of bombardment, and the dependence of the population upon the government for security and guidance, have tended to tear out traditional roots and make the population more susceptible to new ideas, values, and practices. A cohesive political leadership, committed to purposeful change, has certain advantages for carrying out its aims.

Politics: The Front

The front (NLHS, Neo Lao Hak Sat, or Lao Patriotic Front) is the most important open political organization of Lao Communist rule. It serves as the principal mass-mobilizing instrument and transmission belt of the People's Party of Laos (referred to as the PPL or simply the party), which is the policy-making organ. While the party is limited to a relatively small number of carefully selected members, the front is a broad organization which, in the words of a PPL document (LBN-10), "is composed of all progressive persons who wish to resist the imperialists and their lackeys." At the same time, the front is the coordinator for more specialized mass organizations or, as its Secretary-General Phoumi Vongvichit described it in an interview with a German newspaper, "the NLHS is a political organization which unites several anti-imperialist organizations of the people."[1] Describing the relationship of the open front to the clandestine party, one former PL officer used the analogy of a tree: "the Front would be the bark, and the Party its core."[a]

A party training document (LP-24), in typical question-and-answer form, compares the front with the party:

What is the difference between the People's Party of Laos and the Front?

The PPL is the leading force for revolution. The Party has been systematically organized on a strong basis with good discipline. Members are patriotic Lao who are more active and progressive than others. They show determination to fight persistently, and are loyal to the interests of the nation and the people. Our Party, which abides by Marxism-Leninism, is the supreme organization. It has the correct strategy and tactics to struggle for the rights of the poor who are victims of oppression. Through this struggle our country will attain independence and unity.

The Neo Lao Hak Sat is not a party. It is a broad organization that aims at promoting harmonious struggle of the Lao people of all ethnic groups, all classes, all religions, both sexes, and all progressive people against the imperialists and their lackeys. The Front works for the unity of the entire nation, inducing the Lao people to follow the policy of our Party. Our Party plays an important role in all activities of the Neo Lao Hak Sat. However, since the existence of our party is still secret, we camouflage ourselves within the Neo Lao Hak Sat. . . .

The NLHS front, like the National Liberation front in South Vietnam, does not advertise its Communist connections but rather presents itself as a nationalist organization.[2] An East German author who visited Prince Souphanouvong in the summer of 1958, probably in Vientiane, writes that the prince said to him, "We aren't a Communist Party, as people often assert, but supporters of the national liberation movement which abroad is called Pathet Lao." The author states that Souvanna Phouma told him that the NLHS protests against being described as a Communist party, but that its basic ideas and methods are identical to one. Phoumi Vongvichit is quoted in response as saying that "everyone who opposes American domination is labelled a 'Communist.' "[3]

The Pathet Lao front policy follows the Vietnamese Communist doctrine, referred to as the "strategy of [temporary] alliances by stage" (*sach luoc dong minh giai doan*). This doctrine posits leadership of the revolution by a vanguard of workers and peasants, who must attract the less reliable revolutionary elements such as intellectuals, urban students, bourgeoisie, and middle and rich peasants. However, the "class line" must not be abandoned—either by errors of the right or by errors of the left—and once the revolution is victorious, the vanguard must move to the succeeding stage, the consolidation of a "people's democracy."[4]

---

[a]The NLHS transformed itself into a political party to contest the RLG elections in 1958. Hence, both the PPL and the NLHS are often referred to in PL documents as "party" (phak), which has created confusion for some analysts. Soviet interpretations of Lao affairs which we have examined regularly refer to the front as a "party." We have used the term "front" to refer to the NLHS organization, and "party" to refer only to the PPL.

In line with this front strategy, the leadership of the Lao revolution is said to be in the hands of a worker-peasant alliance whose duty it is to attract into the NLHS all "progressive people" who are willing to fight against the imperialists. The North Vietnamese cadre's notebook referred to in the preceding chapter shows that the front strategy defines three political forces in Laos: "the anti-American, the patriotic neutralist, and the anti-revolutionary force." Workers and peasants constitute the anti-American force; feudalists and upper bourgeoisie, with some exceptions, form the antirevolutionary force; a variety of "patriotic Lao" such as intellectuals, students, and national bourgeoisie make up the patriotic neutralist force. The leadership of the revolution, composed of the anti-American force, "should be flexible in order to attract the neutralist force." Once the revolution has succeeded, the leadership must "then move toward the emancipation of the people and the establishment of a people's democracy."

Since the front, as an institution, has adapted to a variety of political circumstances during its two decades of existence, and is a vital element in the administration and control of the zone, we shall briefly discuss some of the major events in Laos which have affected its development.

History of the Front

The First Resistance Congress of Laos was organized by Prince Souphanouvong and other Pathet Lao leaders with Viet Minh encouragement to carry on the struggle against the French in Laos after the dissolution of the Lao Issara in 1949. This congress proclaimed the establishment of the Neo Lao Issara, or Lao Freedom Front, on August 13, 1950. A "Resistance Government," which had overlapping membership with the front, was also established by this congress. The front and resistance government worked closely with the Viet Minh, operating from a headquarters at Tuyen Quang in North Vietnam, until the successful Viet Minh offensive in eastern Laos in 1953 permitted them to establish a base in Laos itself, in the border province of Sam Neua. They extended their influence in that province as well as in Phong Saly, the province that juts into South China and also borders on North Vietnam. The Geneva Conference of 1954 called for the establishment of regroupment areas of Viet Minh and Pathet Lao troops into bases within these two provinces, and directed that Pathet Lao authorities could exercise temporary administration in these areas until the Pathet Lao and Vientiane authorities would agree upon the terms of integration of Pathet Lao personnel into the Royal Lao Government. PL authorities interpreted the decision as meaning that they had control over the entire two provinces, and acted accordingly.[5] Thus, the front's influence in this eastern region of Laos was more firmly planted by 1956, when a tentative agreement was signed.

The agreement for integration of the Pathet Lao organization into a unified government of Laos called for a partial election to the National Assembly, to be held in 1958, in which the Neo Lao Issara were entitled to run candidates. Responding to the new situation, the front transformed itself into a political party, recognized by the Royal Lao Government, to compete for electoral support within a unified political system. Ever since, the front has enjoyed the official status of a political party on the Lao political scene.

Several changes in the organization of the front marked this transformation into a legal political party. On January 6, 1956, at what was termed its First Congress, the front's name was changed from Neo Lao Issara to Neo Lao Hak Sat (NLHS),[b] or Lao Patriotic Front. Its Central Committee was expanded from twenty to forty members.[6] The larger membership of the Central Committee reflected the growth of the front since the first committee was named. Moreover, in preparing for the electoral contest, it made sense to present the new party as an even more broadly based representative of ethnic, tribal, regional, and occupational groups, as well as to reward certain supporters with a mark of distinction as Central Committee members. While such a large committee appeared cumbersome, in fact relatively few veteran leaders, largely PPL members, held the decision-making power within the smaller Executive Committee (sometimes referred to as the Standing Committee). The congress also adopted a new set of statutes for the front.[7] A program setting forth the NLHS political platform committed it to improvement of the economic situation, standard of living, and education of the people. Appealing to the traditional symbols of legitimacy in Laos, it called for protection of the throne and the Buddhist religion as well as the constitution. Its foreign policy favored a government of neutrality which would "proceed toward cultural and economic exchanges" with all countries.

In May 1958, the NLHS party scored a striking success in its first election with the RLG. Of the twenty-one seats available, the NLHS contested ten seats and won nine, and its ally, the Santiphab (Peace and Freedom) party, won four. Among the victorious NLHS candidates were: Souphanouvong, Phoumi Vongvichit, Nouhak Phongsavan, Sithon Kommadam, Phoun Sipraseut, Khamphay Boupa, Khampeng Boupha, and Sisana Sisane. Following the election, the newly elected NLHS National Assemblymen took their seats in Vientiane.

The NLHS electoral victory set off anxiety as well as activity among anti-NLHS political forces. A new right-wing government under Phoui Sananikone came to power in August 1958, along with a new American-supported political party, the CDNI, both hostile to NLHS integration in the government.[8] The deadlock over the modalities of integration of two PL battalions into the Forces Armées Royales (FAR) exacerbated the tensions. Right-wing groups, particularly police and military authorities, exerted a variety of pressures, some

---

[b]Official Lao Communist sources spell the term Neo Lao Haksat. However, some Soviet sources use our preferred spelling that more accurately reflects the several elements entering into the term.

of which are mentioned below, upon the NLHS representatives in Vientiane. Anxiety spread among the NLHS leaders, and they ceased to hold any large meetings. Even smaller meetings were not scheduled on fixed dates.

At a small NLHS meeting in April 1959, an appraisal by Nouhak, at that time an Assemblyman from Sam Neua, suggests how the NLHS leaders saw conditions in Vientiane. He was disturbed by the growing ties between the RLG and the SEATO powers and especially by the arrival of American and Filipino technicians and the mounting supply of American war material. NLHS opposition to these ties, he stated, had stirred the wrath of corrupt RLG politicians who were profiting from this outside aid. NLHS leaders were being subjected to all sorts of intimidation, even arrests and murder. Pressure was being applied to NLHS members to resign from the party. Their newspaper, the *Lao Hak Sat*, was frequently threatened. The RLG was spreading false information that the NLHS opposed religion and the monarchy and that it was a slave of its Communist-bloc allies.

Nouhak evaluated both NLHS and governmental weaknesses. Factionalism, particularly the rivalry between the military strongman Phoumi Nosavan and his opponents, weakened the government. Corruption was rife in the army, the police, and the governmental bureaucracy, and discipline in all three was abominable. The United States, aware of the incompetence of its client, was inclined to act directly within Laos, making the RLG vulnerable to NLHS charges of American domination which repelled the Lao people who did not wish to become an American colony. As for NLHS weaknesses, Nouhak admitted that popular discontent had not brought people into the NLHS camp but had left them noncommittal. Too many cadres were consumed with personal interests and were not active enough in party work. The sense of camaraderie which had existed in the bush had declined, he said, and there was no longer the same brotherly sharing of the rich with the poor.

Whatever its political strategy might have called for, the NLHS was forced to abandon its participation in the RLG in mid-1959, following two events. First, in May, after continual disagreement about the terms of integration of the two PL battalions, FAR troops surrounded and attempted to disarm them. One entire battalion and part of the other escaped to a PL-controlled zone in the east, and subsequently to North Vietnam. Second, RLG authorities imprisoned sixteen NLHS leaders, including the elected Assemblymen, and charged them with treason.[9] Hostilities erupted in July 1959 between governmental and Communist (including NVA) forces and continued intermittently until 1962.

In May 1960, the imprisoned NLHS leaders managed to escape to their home base. Soon afterward, in July 1960, a new "independent government" for Laos was announced, which included:

Prime Minister and Minister of the
   Interior   Souphanouvong

Minister of Foreign Affairs	Phoumi Vongvichit
Minister of Defense	Kaysone Phomvihan
Deputy Minister of Defense	Sithon Kommadam
Minister of Agriculture	Nouhak Phongsavan
Minister of Information	Sisana Sisane
Minister of Labor	Singkapo Chounramany
Minister of Culture	Souk Vongsak

The front transformed itself once again from a legal political party working within the RLG to a revolutionary organization fighting the government. The front's role was now to provide the open political leadership, while the semisecret PPL provided the basic control, for winning over territory and people from the RLG. With the cessation of fighting and the conclusion of the Geneva Agreements in 1962, the NLHS, with North Vietnamese assistance, had spread its domination to at least half the territory of Laos.

The establishment of the tripartite government in Laos in 1962 returned the NLHS once again to participation in a "unified" government. However, though Prince Souphanouvong served as deputy prime minister and Phoumi Vongvichit was a minister in the tripartite government, the NLHS front and its government continued to exercise authority in the areas that the Communist armed forces controlled. During the short period of NLHS participation with the RLG there were no elections for the NLHS to contest. By 1963, relations were once again strained and the NLHS leaders, claiming they had insufficient personal security, quit Vientiane for the NLHS-controlled regions and have not returned.

Since the departure of the NLHS leaders from the Vientiane government, the front has held a second congress in 1964 and a third congress in 1968, both reiterating the hard line adopted in 1963. Expressing itself in a combative mood, the second congress vowed "to struggle against the U.S. imperialists and their followers—the traitors." However, it did not claim to be the sole legitimate government and its ten-point program adopted in 1964 still propagated the theme of national unity, calling for a "correct" implementation of the Geneva Agreements and the other accords reached by the three Lao parties. It insisted upon genuine independence for Laos, demanding an end to American "encroachment," the establishment of diplomatic relations with "various countries on equal footing," and delivery of aid from all countries without strings.[10] Once again, while its core leadership remained the same, the Central Committee was enlarged, this time from forty to sixty members, a measure granting recognition to new leaders in the enlarged population and area controlled by the NLHS.[11]

By the opening of the third congress in November 1968, the gap between the NLHS and RLG had widened. According to its official news agency, the NLHS congress opened in an "atmosphere filled with enthusiasm and joy over the victorious struggle against the U.S. imperialist aggressors and their henchmen."[12] Much of the twelve-point program it adopted followed the same lines as the earlier ten-point program.[13] However, special attention was paid to the "Patriotic Neutralist Forces," the splinter group of erstwhile Kong Le neutralists who had allied themselves with the Pathet Lao. Their leader, Khamsouk Keola, was quoted as having voiced "full support" for the new program and determination "to strengthen the alliance and militant cooperation" between the NLHS and neutralist forces. Also, another new theme since the last congress was the statement that the problems of Laos must be settled by the Lao themselves "on the basis of the 1962 Geneva Agreements and in conformity with the current realities." The United States must stop its bombing in Laos as a precondition for preliminary negotiations among "the Lao themselves."

"Current realities," a theme propounded frequently after the congress, suggested that NLHS gains since the 1962 Geneva Agreements in territory and population control, as well as in political strength, must be recognized. This stress on the need for reopening "the current realities of the situation" taken together with the inflation of the importance of the "patriotic neutralists" at the congress and the denunciation of the neutralists of Prime Minister Souvanna Phouma, indicated an intention of NLHS authorities to claim a larger political role by demanding a share in the coalition government for "their" neutralists. (Although no announcements to this effect were made at the third congress, it is possible that changes were made in the NLHS Central Committee, as in former congresses.)

An important new five-point proposal setting forth the PL's principal peace demands was issued on March 6, 1970 and remained the basis of the PL negotiating position through early 1973, as a cease-fire settlement approached.[c] Following previous statements, the proposal demanded a cessation of American intervention in Laos, and called for a return to the 1962 Geneva agreement. It reaffirmed respect for the throne, and called for general elections to the National Assembly and the establishment of a democratic government of national coalition. The PL's most significant difference with its RLG adversary was over the composition of the government that both agreed should be constituted after a cease-fire. The PL maintained that the tripartite government of national union that had been established by the Geneva Accord of 1962 was dissolved at the time of the abortive coup by Generals Phoumi Nosavan and Siho in 1964, which was followed by a series of cabinet reshuffles. Since then, the PL contended, Souvanna Phouma and his former neutralist colleagues have merged with and become the right and must now be considered simply the "Vientiane party." The center is now constituted, they claimed, by the "Patriotic Neutralists," who are allied with the Pathet Lao. However, the PL position paper left open consideration of additional appointees to the center, of "intellectuals and personalities advocating peace, neutrality, and independence." In addition to a new government, the PL proposal called for the formation of a "political consultative council" (PCC), obviously copying the institution that was to be established in South Vietnam, following the signing of the Paris Agreement on

[c]See Appendix E for the text of this five-point peace proposal.

January 27, 1973. Although the role of the PCC appeared unclear, it was called the highest expression of national unity. The PCC would be formed through consultations and would control and supervise implementation of all agreements among the Lao parties with the assistance of the International Control Commission under terms of the 1962 Geneva Accord. The new government would conduct foreign relations, maintain peace, implement agreement among the parties, receive and distribute foreign aid, and in coordination with the PCC, prepare for elections to the new National Assembly to form a permanent coalition government.

Administration: The Front and the Government

There is a dual system of government and administration at each echelon of authority in the Pathet Lao zone. One line runs from the central headquarters of the front and the other from the central government. The front (termed the neo) acts as the NLHS public·spokesman, sends delegations abroad and receives foreign representatives, directs internal political programs such as the mass-mobilizing activities, formulates broad public policy, and generally supervises administration. The government, though it appears to be a coordinate branch, actually works under the guidance of the neo, merely conducting the day-to-day administrative activities of the zone. This branch has the normal departments of government, each of which has a front counterpart, such as national defense, foreign affairs, health, interior, education and propaganda, and economic and finance.

The supreme headquarters for both, frequently referred to as "the center" by PL cadres (a term also commonly used by the Vietnamese), was located at Ban Nakay Neua in Sam Neua Province in a cave complex with office space for some 500 personnel. An American reporter who visited Prince Souphanouvong said that the headquarters had been hewn from nine natural caves and transformed into enlarged caverns that housed hospitals, workshops, offices of the leaders, and even a hostel for foreign journalists. The greatest problem within the caverns, he reported, was not bombs, but moisture.[14] For protection against air strikes, some high-ranking NLHS leaders, including Prince Souphanouvong, live in rooms in the caves.

There are Vietnamese advisers in both branches. An NLHS liaison office in Hanoi (in addition to the PPL "Office 98" there) is thought to be responsible for Lao receiving training in North Vietnam, and some Lao officials intermittently visit nearby North Vietnamese authorities, on whom they depend for guidance, supplies, and military support. There has been an NLHS liaison office in Vientiane which has maintained contact with the RLG, the International Control Commission, foreign embassies, and visitors. The office was headed by a veteran Pathet Lao member, Colonel Sot Petrasy, and guarded by about a 100-man Lao People's Liberation Army unit.

The front and government have a subordinate structure similar to the one described for the party. (See Figures 3-1 and 3-2, showing the NLHS command structure and location of its headquarters.) The supreme headquarters at Sam Neua, assisted by its subordinate South Laos regional tactical headquarters located in northern Savannakhet Province, has four subordinate regional subdivisions and below this are sixteen provincial headquarters directing districts, cantons and villages. At each level there is a neo chief and an administrative chief, each of whom presides over a committee of members who are individually responsible for specific functional tasks. While the neo echelon is unique to the NLHS system, the administrative structure from the province to the village

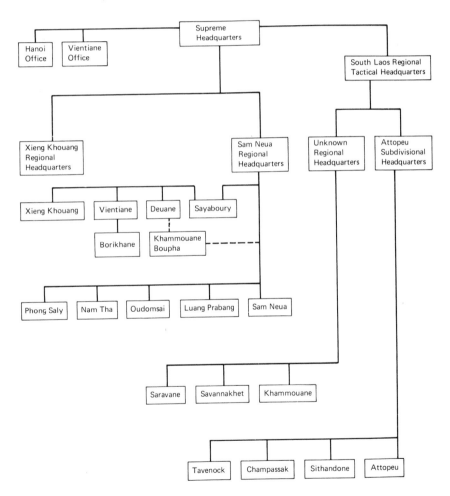

Figure 3-1. The Neo Lao Hak Sat (NLHS) Command Structure

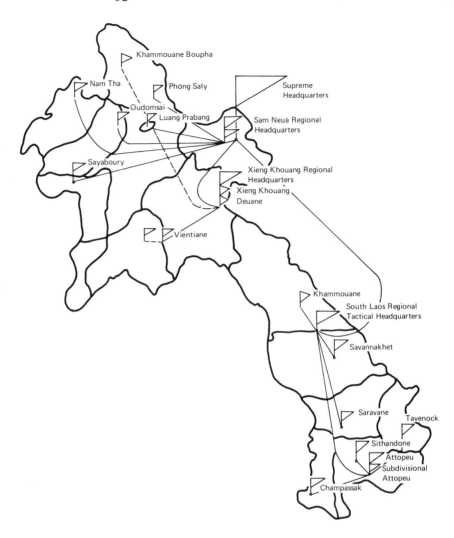

Figure 3-2. Neo Lao Hak Sat Command Structure Locations

resembles that of the RLG. A comparison of the PL province names and boundaries (shown in Figure 3-3) with those of the RLG (shown in Figure 3-4) reveals a number of differences: for example, the PL authorities have not accepted certain RLG provincial changes (such as the creation by the RLG of Vapikhamthong Province); they have different names for certain provinces (such as Nam Tha for the RLG Houa Khong Province); different boundaries for similarly named provinces (Luang Prabang); and they have several provinces with

Figure 3-3. Neo Lao Hak Sat Provinces

names and boundaries different from those of the RLG (Taven Ock and Udomsai). The two maps in Figure 3-5 approximate the changes in territorial control by the PL and the RLG in 1962 and 1970.

There are two elements of the dissident neutralists:[15] the Deuanist neutralists in Xieng Khouang Province and the Khammouane Boupha neutralists in Phong Saly Province, bordering on China. The Deuanist forces had occupied the Plain

Figure 3-4. The Administrative Divisions of the Royal Lao
Government (RLG)

of Jars from the time of their split with the Kong Le neutralists in March 1963
until mid-1969, when the plain was taken by RLG Meo forces, led by General
Vang Pao. The Deuanists moved their headquarters to Nong Het, in eastern
Xieng Khouang Province. When North Vietnamese and Pathet Lao troops
reoccupied the Plain of Jars in February 1970, it is possible that the Deuanists
transferred headquarters to their former location. The Khammouane Boupha
neutralist headquarters has been located in the provincial capital of Phong Saly.

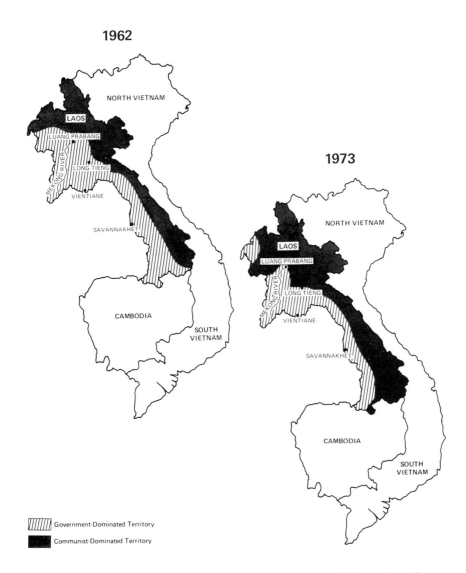

Figure 3-5. Changing Areas of Control (Approximate)

While the lines of authority are not clear, the Khammouane Boupha neutralists serve within the command structure either under Colonel Deuane or under the Sam Neua regional headquarters (see Figures 2-1 and 2-2). Actually Khammouane Boupha has appeared to retain a measure of independence from PL controls, perhaps because he has maintained closer relations with the Chinese Communists than have either the Deuanists or the NLHS command structure.

The administrative province chief (chao khoueng) normally has a deputy and a committee of seven to nine members, each with responsibility over offices such as police, military affairs, economic affairs, public works and transportation, education, arts and culture, and propaganda and census. Some instructions are sent directly to him, by radio or pouch, from the superior administrative echelon. He communicates orders to his subordinate district chiefs (chao muongs) by personal meetings, held about once a month, and by written orders. However, the front chief (neo khoueng) holds the real authority. His office, though generally having fewer personnel, essentially duplicates that of the chao khoueng, with a deputy and committee members responsible for certain activities. The neo khoueng handles political affairs for the province, working through the subordinate neo muongs, and also supervises the work of the chao khoueng.

An account of administration in a PL district of Luang Prabang Province, from the perspective of a former PL chao muong whom we interviewed(A-16), provides a sample of governmental activities that are generally repeated in other PL-controlled areas. A chart drawn by the chao muong describes the provincial administrative pattern in 1964 (see Figure 3-6). Though the basic structure remains the same today, there are variations from province to province and undoubtedly, changes since 1964.

When Viet Minh troops accompanied by a few Lao guerrillas arrived in his home region in 1953, our source, who had been a farmer, was drawn into the Neo Lao Issara organization. He rose to the position of chief of a fifty-man local militia unit by the end of hostilities in 1954. Though he had little formal schooling he was intelligent and as the son of a former tasseng (canton chief) had an inclination for administration. Inasmuch as he had achieved recognition as a militia leader and the Communist forces controlled his region it was natural for him to move into the PL bureaucracy. In the decade following the Geneva Agreements he gained experience in jobs at the canton, district, and provincial levels, at first in his home area and later in the more firmly PL-controlled areas of Phong Saly and Sam Neua. In his description of his work, three important tasks of all PL cadres are evident: recruit soldiers, collect rice, and make propaganda. In 1963, at age thirty-six, he was appointed to be a chao muong in Luang Prabang Province, near his birthplace. While his promotions had been steady, they had not been rapid and his tasks were largely administrative, not political (except for the requirement, demanded of all cadres, to make propaganda). He was respected for his administrative ability but he felt he was not fully trusted because of his "middle-class origins." Following differences with his superiors, he was discharged from office in 1964, and two years later he defected to the RLG. Probably because of the paucity of qualified administrative personnel in the Communist zone, the Pathet Lao often retain lower-ranking officials of the previous regime when they take over a new area. This was confirmed by a number of our interviewees. A footnote in a collection of Lao

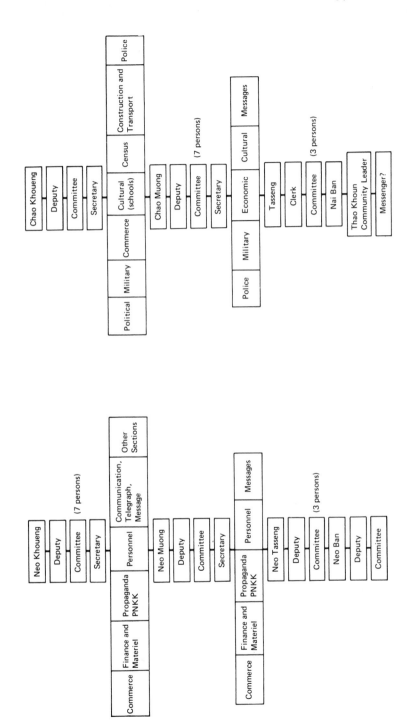

Figure 3-6. The Provincial Administrative Structure

Communist short stories issued by the NLHS, for example, states: "After liberation the Pathet Lao maintained at their posts a number of notables serving the former regime."[16] A similar policy applies to teachers and medical personnel.[17]

Our informant continued that as chao muong he was confined largely to administrative duties. He received instructions from the neo muong, located just 200 yards from his own headquarters, and from the chao khoueng at the echelon above him. Unlike him, two of his subordinates, a clerk and a muong committeeman, were party members and reported on his activities. Though they did not reveal themselves as members, he knew they belonged to the party because they were called out for clandestine meetings from time to time and because certain of his mistakes, which could not have been known outside the confines of his office, were raised at neo criticism sessions.

In discussing administrative jurisdictions with us he pointed out that only conflicts that could not be settled at the muong level by the neo were to be referred to the khoueng for decisions. As an example, he recounted:

When I was chao muong I allowed people in the muong to travel about from village to village in the territory of the royal government on their business. Someone reported this to the neo. A criticism session was held at the muong level. I was told by the neo that I should not have done this—it was not within my responsibility. The neo himself had never received orders from the neo khoueng to allow people to travel in royal government areas. He knew, too, that I had not received orders from the chao khoueng to permit such travel. I admitted that I had committed a fault. As a result, the problem was settled at the muong level. The neo muong submitted a report on my case to the new khoueng.

Since the district had an ethnically mixed population, Lao Loum, Lao Theung, and Meo cadres served in positions of authority. The neo muong and his deputy were Lao Theung of the Khmu group and the chao muong's own deputy was a Khmu. At the khoueng level, the neo was a Lao Loum and his deputy a White Tai; the chao khoueng was a Lao Loum, his deputy a Meo, and most of the people in the office were Lao Theung. Ethnic group issues would normally be handled within the administration by a representative of the appropriate group. Ethnic problems were not difficult to handle within the PL administration, he said. Lack of education among the Lao Theung cadres was not a problem, he said, because:

Problems were discussed and decisions made together. During a discussion, everyone expressed his opinion. If his opinion was agreeable to the policy of the party, everyone would follow his opinion, no matter if he were a Kha or a Lao Loum. It is more important that a person's opinion be in conformity with the party than that he is a Lao Loum and educated.

He noted that the Lao Theung cadres at the khoueng level were experienced and competent:

All of them proved capable of operating in accordance with center's policy. Some of them might have had a low level of education, but they had worked for center for a long time and had a great deal of experience. They had been appointed to important province positions. Someone with a good education but not experience with the center would be considered a man with only theory but not the capability of carrying out policies, and would not be appointed by center.

As for Lao Loum resentment toward obeying Lao Theung:

This is also not a problem. Most people believe that anyone who is appointed as a chief is authorized to lead them, and they are supposed to obey. If his orders conform to the principles of justice, most people accept them.

The dual front-government administration described above continues to the lowest echelon, the village (ban), where there is a front chief (neo ban) and administrative chief (nai ban). (In some villages, and even at higher echelons, the two offices are sometimes filled by one person.) The nai ban handles the day-to-day administration of the village; the neo ban, besides guiding his colleagues, handles political affairs, particularly the mass organizations to be described presently. A third important member of the village committee is the cadre for military affairs, charged with organizing the men of the village into a militia for guard duty, guerrilla activity, and other military tasks.

A great effort is made at every administrative echelon to bring people into a variety of special-interest (often referred to in Communist literature as "mass") organizations.[18] A concentrated campaign is applied at the village level, with the aim of drawing almost every able-bodied individual into at least one of three organizations: a men's organization, a women's organization, and a youths' organization. Girls from fifteen to twenty-five and men from fifteen to thirty-five are each taken into their own branch of the youths' organization. Refugees from the Pakse region, in describing the major thrust by NLHS cadres to organize their youths, reported that the neo muong sent a youth-training adviser to the villages, and the neo ban would often act as president of the organization. Since a large proportion of the men in most areas are in the army, the young women's organization frequently assumes the greatest importance in the village. The girls prepare small gifts and food and work at other schemes to lift the morale of the soldiers. Political indoctrination is given at all meetings, with encouragement to teach the lessons to others, and a self-criticism session is conducted prior to the close of the meeting. The young men's organization follows the same pattern but other assignments are distributed, such as guard duty, porterage or messenger service, or control of travelers' passes.

The organizations are linked together in zonewide associations, and rallies, heavily laden with political propaganda, are held from time to time at the canton, the district, and even the province level.[19] Special organizations are developed for particular target groups, and statements on behalf of these organizations are issued. For example, a PL radio broadcast in Lao proclaimed that "the Laotian Buddhist Association supports the NLHS Manifesto of 1965 and calls on monks in the RLG areas to struggle against the United States."[20]

Another Lao Communist organizational feature, aimed at embracing all families in their zone (though they don't achieve this) is the interfamily group. Following the Vietnamese Communist technique, usually about five families are linked under the leadership of an elder in whom the village authorities have some confidence. The family groups are promoted as associations for mutual coopera-tion but, although they may serve this end in some cases, they seem principally an additional method of control and intelligence gathering. Family chiefs are expected to know the activities of their members and to cooperate in mobilizing them for tasks imposed by the village authorities.

Propaganda and Controls

Social control in the PL zone depends upon a mix of persuasion and coercion. Claiming that they are fighting a "people's war," the Lao Communist leaders believe it is important for simple people not only to understand the struggle but to embrace it with conviction. Propaganda is the chief instrument used to promote this frame of mind. However, obedience, even without wholehearted acceptance, is fundamental. Thus, controls are also important to promote compliance and to punish deviance.

In their propaganda the Lao Patriotic Front seeks legitimacy for its authority both by discrediting its adversaries and by attempting to convince people of the justice of its cause. Almost all NLHS institutions, civilian and military, are required to contribute to the propaganda campaign. Part of each cadre's political indoctrination is his duty to carry the "political truth" to each person whose path he crosses. Every occasion—local festival, religious celebration, national holiday—must be used to trumpet NLHS policy. All associations, particularly the youths', men's and women's organizations, are politicized, and each member is called upon to carry NLHS propaganda themes to others. As our description of the party, front, and governmental organization has shown, propaganda depart-ments are placed throughout the entire organizational structure, from the center down through each administrative echelon to the village. The official NLHS newspaper, the *Lao Hak Sat*, was reported to have a daily circulation in 1959 of up to 15,000 copies (present circulation unknown). There is a news agency (Khao Sone Pathet Lao) and a radio outlet (Radio Pathet Lao) both listing Sam Neua Province as their source of origin. Although we do not know the extent of Radio Pathet Lao's audience, from interviews we know it can be heard in Vientiane and other Mekong Valley towns.

Various forms of mobile propaganda teams, often armed, operate in PL-con-trolled and contested zones. Recent refugees from Xieng Khouang Province have described an important effort there over the past three years carried out by "The Awakening Group" (Khana Puk Luk).[21] This group, based at the provincial level and consisting of "outsiders," meaning cadres not necessarily from the immediate area, are so important they appear almost as a third branch of government (in addition to the neo and governmental branches, or a fourth, if one thinks of the Vietnamese advisers as a separate branch). The group's goal, though it was not yet achieved, is to place two cadres in each village. Following the Vietnamese Communist practice, these cadres are trained to practice the "four togethers" with the people: eat together, work together, discuss together, and assist each other. In addition to their propaganda tasks, these cadres provide political surveillance and leadership in community development projects.

The propaganda effort is, of course, directed at particular target groups. For example, in addition to their offerings in the Lao language, radio broadcasts are made in some of the ethnic group languages such as Meo and Black Tai. Special propaganda teams are organized with minority members. A document found in Xieng Khouang Province, dated January 14, 1968, shows that thirty-three Buddhist monks were assigned to cantons and districts "to preach revolutionary ethics ... to protect Buddhism, to revive the real morality, to explain the revolutionary tasks to the people, and to resist the psychological warfare of the American imperialists and their reactionary lackeys." In an NLHS publication, *Worthy Daughters and Sons of the Lao People*, issued in 1966 there is a story showing what we know from other sources, that PL agents often circulate within RLG territory for economic transactions or to make propaganda. In this account, a propagandist enters a Royal Lao Government village during the celebration on Buddha's birthday and addresses the crowd, "denouncing the crimes of the American aggressors and their valets." He reports, "I expounded the line of the Neo Lao Haksat, which struggles for peace, neutrality, independence, national unification, democracy and prosperity.[22] Another NLHS book contains this passage, "The old man immediately sent his daughter for a Neo Lao Haksat cadre working underground in Pung village. He suggested that liberation troops be sent to the plain for ambush."[23]

As in any system, law and the courts are means of social control. The NLHS combine traditional practices with certain Communist techniques in their legal system. Refugees from Xieng Khouang Province report that minor offenses like petty theft are adjudicated at the village level, often by means of a self-criticism session by the accused before members of a village or tasseng committee. For more serious offenses, a "people's" court may be convened, where the accused reads a confession before assembled villagers and suggests the punishment he should receive. His statement, apparently prepared by propaganda cadres, is applauded by the villagers, and the accused is taken off for punishment. Offenses defined as serious include attempts to escape, profiteering, adultery, and passing information to RLG agents. The punishment may be reduced if the authorities are convinced that the prisoner has repented and, in some cases, where the family has invested a significant labor contribution.[24]

Refugees from PL-controlled areas in South Laos point out that the village chief is responsible for local law enforcement. He may request military assistance to arrest a culprit in the case of crimes he cannot handle with his own resources. A village people's court deals with some offenses. Pathet Lao authorities do not speak of jail sentences but in place of traditional punishment send villagers off "to study." There are no prisons, state PL cadres, but only places to separate "students" (offenders) from patriotic citizens. Those who commit civil crimes are assigned teachers from the khoueng's (provincial) office, and those committing offenses against the military are assigned military teachers. A former PL village chief from an area near Muong Phine in southern Laos reported that there were two types of discipline under the people's court system in his region. For the most serious crimes, authorities announce that the "student" has defected to the enemy, meaning that he has been executed. For less serious crimes, the offender is sentenced to a "period of study," during which he is confined to a small area, perhaps 20 yards square, where his teacher comes daily to instruct him for a period that may last from one to two months. The student must confess his life history and learn proper revolutionary morality from his teacher. If the teacher, in consultation with other authorities, believes that the student has repented, he is released.[25]

The widespread placement of secret agents is another NLHS technique for inducing obedience. Agents are infiltrated into enemy and contested territory as well as PL-controlled areas deemed strategic, to collect military intelligence and to report on the political attitudes of individuals who are important in the community. A six-month plan of the PPL organization bureau for Xieng Khouang Province contained the following instructions:

Try to establish political bases in every newly-liberated area . . . try to infiltrate our well-trained agents into the rear areas of the enemy in order to set up our bases. We must have at least one well-trained agent in each district at the rear of the enemy.[26]

Earlier RLG studies of the Pathet Lao movement have described an organization of the "kene san" (faithful agents). These kene san were described as agents interspersed throughout the political administrative hierarchy to report secretly, through kene san channels, upon activities of functionaries within the NLHS system, as well as upon behavior of individuals within the population. These agents were presumably unaware of each other and often skipped a level of the administrative hierarchy in their reporting to a superior cadre in order to preserve secrecy. A former PL cadre stated that the previously discussed Internal Defense Organization has taken over the function of checking on the behavior of party personnel.

A former NVA adviser (B-9) to a PL battalion whom we interviewed recognized the device as an inportation from North Vietnam (where the practice was known as *trung kien*). From his experience in Laos, he said secret agents are assigned to contested zones to report on target groups such as village chiefs, local administrative officials, and families with sons in the Forces Armées Royales. A former PL district chief (A-16), in describing the kene san from his experience, confirmed this account. He described the kene san as agents whom the PL authorities would first contact in preparing to seize a village.

These are people who had been trained and considered trustworthy by the Pathet Lao authorities. They would contact these people to find out the real situation in the village. In other words kene san are loyal supporters in the village—there might be two or three men.

A PL document (LBN-3) prescribing political tactics for contested areas, adds, "the existence of kene san must be absolutely concealed." Another document, in an evaluation of political activities, notes that in the "development of underground agents we have attained 50 percent."

The effect of this variety of clandestine agents throughout the PL and contested zones understandably tends to make people cautious in their political behavior. As in any society with large numbers of spies, a sense of mistrust is created. We have no means of measuring the intensity or pervasiveness of fear caused by the knowledge that such agents exist, but we know from our talks with former PL personnel and refugees from PL areas that this feeling is a common grievance. It is clear that the PL practice of sending secret agents into contested and enemy-controlled areas makes people wary of enemy agents in their own areas. An NLHS document dated January 19, 1969, concerning the duties of cadres working in a newly liberated area cautions them to "wipe out the secret agents of the enemy. Suppress all reactionaries who are still trying to hinder us from establishing our roots."

Another control established in all PL areas is the restriction on personal movement. While enforcement of travel controls varies from region to region, each area has a system of passes and establishes checkpoints to regulate the movement of inhabitants and to scrutinize strangers in the area. In some areas soldiers are required to have permits from their political sections for travel outside the limits of their military unit. In some jurisdictions canton chiefs must sign passes whereas in others only district chiefs may issue them.

An Assessment

The Political and Administrative Record

Our foregoing history of the front has shown that over the past score of years the Pathet Lao movement has developed, with critical Vietnamese assistance, from a small insurgent movement to a countergovernment dominating more than two thirds of the territory and more than one third of the population. This expansion must be largely attributed to military means, with the North Vietnamese bearing the major burden. Nevertheless, the PL authorities, operating under extremely difficult conditions, have shown a degree of competence in political and administrative organization that is surprising for Laos; they have mobilized a significant segment of the population of their zone into a variety of organizations, and they have developed the front and administrative apparatus to exercise control in their zone. From examining their internal documents we get the impression that the leaders of the Lao Patriotic Front have a feeling of growth. In good Communist fashion, their own assessments and, even more, those of their Vietnamese mentors dwell more upon their weaknesses than their strengths, but this has proved a useful self-correcting device, prodding them to improve their capabilities.

Our account has shown that the NLHS has been a flexible instrument of policy. During the brief periods of accommodation with the Royal Lao Government it has served as the open political party. In the one relatively free election in 1958, the only contest at the polls against their RLG adversaries, the NLHS achieved a striking success. During the larger segment of its history, when Laos has been under de facto partition, the NLHS has served in the more familiar role in Communist systems of the political front, acting as a mobilizer and coordinator of open political and mass organizations.

The variety of special-interest organizations introduced by the PL authorities, with Vietnamese guidance, have drawn the bulk of the population in the PL zone into some association. These associations have provided a means through which the PL could transmit political indoctrination, and they have been useful for assigning work tasks to certain groups, such as young men, young women, and farmers. Thus, this organizational effort helps in eroding the parochialisms of the diverse peoples in the PL zone and integrating them into a larger political framework.

The Pathet Lao formula for administrative development, in giving first priority to the creation of dedicated, disciplined cadres, has produced a new kind of administrator in Laos. PL cadres have been inculcated with a doctrine that combines nationalism with Marxism-Leninism. The doctrine has the asset of laying out goals at the top and structuring tasks for subordinate echelons to execute. For achieving political change this planning method has advantages over the traditional Lao practice of taking things as they come, more common on the RLG side. Stable political leadership, giving continuity of guidance to the lower-level cadres, has been another PL administrative asset. We have had many indications, even from refugees unsympathetic to the PL system, that the cadres are highly regarded for their hard work and lack of corruption. At the same time, we note reports of their narrowness, severity, and rigidity. Our evidence does not permit us to comment on the trends in morale among the PL political and administrative cadres. As for the top leadership, we see no signs of cracks in their will.

The competence of the PL administrative organization varies widely from region to region. Clearly, an effective organization does not flow through all of the boxes in the charts we have presented. Internal documents point to a great shortage of competent cadres. Some posts on the charts are not filled and some cadres fulfill several functions. The organization seems best developed near the central headquarters, in Sam Neua. In many areas the tribes are ruled by traditional patterns and are only loosely tied to the PL center by bargaining between PL emissaries and local chiefs. We believe these traditional patterns are eroding as youths are recruited and indoctrinated into the PL system.

The PL have been more successful, it appears, than their RLG adversary in creating linkages between the top leadership and the village base. In the RLG system the district chief (chao muong) represents the cutoff point of "the government"; below him, at the canton (tasseng) and village (ban), leadership is drawn from local inhabitants. Seldom do these villagers rise through the RLG system into the governmental structure. By contrast, the PL system offers a greater outlet for talented and ambitious youths, especially poor rural boys, including minority tribesmen, to acquire training and rise through the echelons. Thus, a centralized system functions in which villages are integrally linked to the center, meaning that the leaders can reward and punish, demand and expect compliance with orders, even at the local level.

Inasmuch as we have pointed out the critical role of the North Vietnamese in PL development, we should note other consequences of that support. The PL alliance with the North Vietnamese has been a crucial element, as we have shown, in producing the bipolarization of Laos. Further, U.S. policy in Laos has been inspired principally by U.S. fear of North Vietnamese expansion, and, whether the danger is real or imagined, PL dependence upon the North Vietnamese has been used to justify both the massive support, seen in Lao terms, to the RLG and the U.S. bombing of the PL zone.

More bomb tonnage has been dropped upon Laos, it appears, than on any other country in history. Perhaps the most serious consequence of the U.S. bombing for the Pathet Lao movement has been the flight of thousands of residents. Deputy Assistant Secretary of State William H. Sullivan in testimony on April 22, 1971, before the Senate Judiciary Subcommittee on Refugees (Senator Edward M. Kennedy, Chairman) reported that over 700,000 residents of Laos had been displaced at least once since 1962.[27] A large majority of these refugees are former residents of territory now under PL control.

Our concern here is with the implications of the bombing, and particularly the flight of refugees, for the politics and administration of the PL zone. Clearly the massive damage and dislocation wreaked by this bombardment placed a burden upon the PL administrative apparatus. The distribution of rice will serve as an example of the heavy labor levies that were imposed by wartime conditions. The PL authorities had to collect rice, either by taxes or imports (on the basis of loans, gifts, or exchange), largely from North Vietnam, and distribute it, especially to the troops. Since vehicle and animal transportation were scarce, villagers had to be organized to transport rice from collection to distribution points. Though porterage duty varied from region to region and depended upon seasonal needs, inhabitants of all PL areas had to perform this onerous duty. One report based on interviews with refugees from Xieng Khouang Province stated that porterage was "the single most unpopular aspect of life under the Pathet Lao." "Short trips" were required of almost all able-bodied persons, men and women. One "long trip," normally thirty days of hauling, not including the rest days or the return trip, was generally demanded once yearly.[28]

The refugee exodus has created a severe manpower shortage. Thus, in the same manner as in South Vietnam, the Communists have been deprived of a constituency. Though all population estimates must be regarded as tentative, the North Vietnamese cadre's notebook referring to early 1968 stated that there were 700,000 people—a figure which seems reasonable—living in "the liberated zone." With the serious depletion of the manpower pool, a heavier burden must be placed upon those who stay.

Lastly, how does the PL system compare with that of the RLG in administrative and political effectiveness? Though our data on the technical competence and efficiency of the PL cadres are slim and we have not focused our study upon the RLG, we shall hazard a few comments. Our impression is that on the Royal Lao Government side there is a higher level of technological development. Largely as a result of U.S. aid, RLG technicians have probably had more training and experience in dealing with telecommunication, radio, and automotive equipment. Some RLG personnel have learned to fly transport and fighter planes. Though both sides are poor by outside standards, RLG ministries are more elaborate and, drawing heavily upon U.S. resources and logistic assistance, have developed a larger technical capacity to mount service activities in such fields as agriculture and public works. The RLG bureaucracy probably has a higher level of formal education. On the other hand, the Pathet Lao have a larger capacity, as well as the inclination, to disseminate propaganda and maintain control; and in political organization the PL show a significant lead. If PL cadres are less educated and technologically competent, they are more infused with commitment to a cause and to hard work, and they have a considerably higher reputation for honesty than their RLG counterparts.

Clearly, both sides are heavily dependent upon external support for their present level of capability. If this support were withdrawn from both, we have no doubt that the competence of each would drastically decline. However, if only one external power removed its support, the balance in this comparison would obviously tip in favor of the Lao side that retained foreign assistance.

Public Attitudes Toward Pathet Lao Authority

Finally, what judgment can be made about the population's attitude toward PL rule? Because of the paucity of data, we emphasize the tentativeness of our conclusions.

As we have pointed out, thousands have fled the PL zone for a number of reasons. Unquestionably, bombing has been a major contributor, direct or indirect, to the exodus. As in South Vietnam, one heard, on one hand, that the Lao refugees were "voting with their feet," fleeing oppressive Communist rule; on the other hand, the claim was made that the refugees were fleeing U.S. bombardment. Although we have insufficient data to judge to what degree each of these two elements of the "mix" was responsible for the exodus, we are convinced that the latter was a principal cause. The destruction and the fear caused by the bombing were enormous. Bombs did not fall on the RLG side, and there were relief supplies and medical attention for refugees, provided through the U.S. Agency for International Development, undoubtedly in larger quantities than on the PL side. On the other hand, life was extremely difficult in the PL zone: the burdens of duties of porterage and other corvée labor were heavy; taxes were high and rice was scarce; most able-bodied men and some women were conscripted for fighting; movement was tightly controlled; underground agents monitored behavior; and people had to devote much time in organizations listening to monotonous propaganda.

An important question is the attitude of the population toward North Vietnamese presence in the PL zone. The North Vietnamese were able to camouflage their role somewhat by minimizing their troop contact with the local population and requiring advisers to work with discretion through Lao counter-parts rather than deal directly with the population. A report of interviews with refugees from Xieng Khouang Province, for example, notes that there was widespread ignorance among them about the extensive Vietnamese activities. Few villagers had direct contact with the North Vietnamese and, as most put it, the cadres "didn't let themselves be seen."[29]

Nevertheless, antipathy toward the PL relationship with the North Viet-namese was aroused, according to the North Vietnamese cadre's notebook. An entry evaluating the "situation of the Lao masses" states that "the peoples' political understanding is vague and poor. They think that the Pathet Lao are traitors who are selling their country to the Vietnamese." The blame for this state of mind was attributed to the "enemy scheme aimed at creating friction among the people." A characteristic corrective was therefore ordered: "We must indoctrinate the people to make them aware who are their friends and foes." This task will not be easy, an entry reveals, since the people are "passive" and have "an inferiority complex."

While we are skeptical that either the RLG or PL authorities attract a strong, positive commitment from the population, we have the impression—though admittedly our evidence is thin—that in this respect the PL authorities have been more successful with the Lao Theung population than have the RLG. Few tribal groups have had representation in RLG policy-making circles, and practically no hill tribe people, until recently, have been employed by the government.[30] In contrast, internal documents reveal that within their limited resources NLHS authorities have been engaged in a concerted campaign to bring ethnic groups, particularly their youths, into PL national life by offering opportunities equivalent to those for the lowland Lao.

It is not surprising that refugees who flee to the RLG zone should express antipathy toward PL rule. Regarding the attitudes of those who remain, we have little concrete data. Peasants do not appear to look upon the PL system with terror. While the process of "reeducation" for deviants is not a pleasant one, it does not seem to be regarded as brutal or terroristic. We do not believe that people give strong support to either the PL or the RLG authorities—it seems unrealistic to expect the peasantry of Laos to have strong feelings for any central government. Even though PL cadres may not have endeared themselves to the villagers, the villagers hold them in respect and many admire their industriousness and incorruptibility. Probably more important politically is a government's ability to impose authority upon the population. In this respect, the PL system has a more impressive record than that of the RLG.

4 The Pathet Lao Fighting Forces

The army, known since October 1965 as the Lao People's Liberation Army (LPLA), may be the single most significant Pathet Lao institution. Historically, it has the longest tenure; founded officially on January 20, 1949, it antedates the party, the front, and the government. It is the largest PL organization, with some 35,000 troops in the fall of 1972. Though the party leads the revolutionary struggle, the army probably makes the largest impact on the life of the inhabitants of the PL-controlled zone. In this chapter we describe the growth and structure of the LPLA and such aspects of military life as recruitment and training. Our analysis does not deal with strategy, tactics, operations, or other primarily military issues; rather we seek to examine the LPLA as an important institution within the political, administrative, and social life of the Pathet Lao zone.

Growth of the PL Fighting Forces

The guerrilla bands of Lao soldiers who were organized to fight against the French in the late 1940s, particularly those in Eastern Laos who were guided by Viet Minh cadres, became the nucleus for the future Lao People's Liberation Army (LPLA).[1] These bands served with Viet Minh units in Laos mostly as propagandists, guides, porters, and local agents. Official PL mythology cites a more impressive record for the Lao Issara Armed Forces, as they were known before 1954, claiming that they carried out the "task of fighting and ousting the French colonialists . . . [and] overthrowing the puppet traitors."[2] By contrast, a French governmental study of Laos notes that the number of PL "maquis" did not exceed two to three hundred up to 1953.[3] A North Vietnam cadre's notebook, in an entry acknowledging the contributions of the Viet Minh to the formation of the Lao Issara, stated that the "revolution originated from the outside," and the "armed forces were also formed from outside." By the signing of the Geneva Agreements in July 1954, the PL numbers were estimated to range from 1,500 to 3,000 troops.

A campaign of recruitment continued after Geneva, especially in the PL-controlled provinces of Sam Neua and Phong Saly, and by the fall of 1957 when an integration arrangement was tentatively agreed on by Prince Souphanouvong and Souvanna Phouma, PL troop strength had reached some 6,000. The integration agreement called for two PL battalions to be integrated into the Forces Armées

Royales (FAR), the size of which was set at 23,615 men,[4] and the remaining PL troops were to be demobilized. In an atmosphere of political suspicion between the parties, integration was delayed by a dispute over the grades that the top-level PL officers would receive. It appears that PL officers, who had less formal training than their FAR counterparts, had been rapidly promoted in anticipation of the merger. Impatient with the deadlock, the FAR surrounded the two Pathet Lao battalions. A part of one battalion was captured, but the remainder escaped, as did the entire other battalion, subsequently fleeing to North Vietnam. These troops, together with those who had not been demobilized, were regrouped and retrained, and they then served as cadres who recruited others. In the summer of 1959 an offensive led by North Vietnamese troops gave impetus to these recruiting activities.

By the time of the Kong Le coup in August 1960, the PL armed forces had grown to an estimated 9,000 troops. The coup and the consequent turbulence in the royal army and government provided a windfall to the Pathet Lao, who were given, or seized, arms from the royal army stocks. When fighting broke out again, following the countercoup of Phoumi Nosavan, the Pathet Lao forces were further strengthened by the Soviet equipment and supplies which began to pour in. The North Vietnamese, who controlled the Soviet assistance, used it principally for themselves, but they also distributed a share to the Pathet Lao forces. The offensive in the spring of 1961, led by North Vietnamese shock troops with Pathet Lao and Kong Le participation, spread Communist domination to new regions in central and southern Laos. Encouraged by the momentum of this success, and with a larger population under their domination, the PL increased their forces to some 16,000 by the cease-fire of May 1961. Following the cease-fire, the PL had expanded their forces to an estimated 19,500 by the conclusion of the Geneva negotiations in July 1962.

With a respite in the hostilities provided by the Geneva Agreements of 1962, the Pathet Lao authorities, who now controlled more than half the area of the country, had time, and North Vietnamese support, both to consolidate their forces and to continue their recruitment campaign. Their force strength rose steadily, reaching 20,000 in November 1964; 25,000 in June 1965; 33,000 in April 1967; and over 48,000 in 1970, organized in battalions of infantry, armor, artillery, antiaircraft, and engineers. By the fall of 1972, PL strength had dropped to 35,000, according to U.S. estimates reflecting the intense fighting and accompanying heavy casualties since 1970.[5] The areas controlled by the Pathet Lao and by the Royal Army in 1970 are shown in Figure 4-1.

The North Vietnamese, as we have pointed out, played a key role in the creation of the PL armed forces and have subsequently provided critical guidance and assistance to their growth. On the battlefield, the NVA—with some 50,000 troops in Laos in 1970 increasing to 63,000 in the fall of 1972,

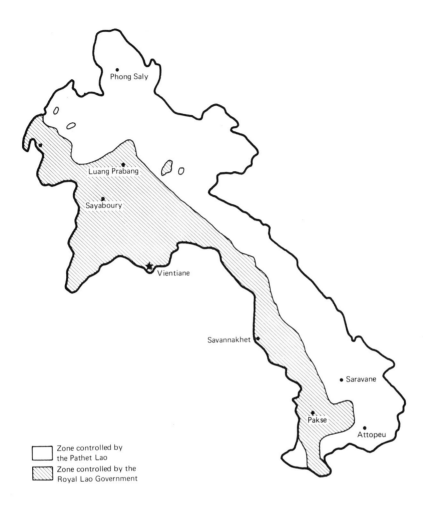

Figure 4-1. Areas of Control (Approximate), 1970

according to U.S. estimates—has generally provided the military thrust, whereas the LPLA has more often been in a support role, moving in to consolidate control and deal with the local population. The territorial gains of the Lao Communist movement must be seen, therefore, as a product of this joint NVA and LPLA effort. In the following section, so as to provide a context for our examination of the LPLA, we shall describe briefly the nature of the war in Laos since the collapse of the 1962 Geneva Agreements.

The Recent War: An Overview

In 1963, when relations ruptured and fighting resumed between the RLG and the Pathet Lao, a pattern of hostilities emerged in which it appeared that both sides had adopted implicit ground rules. According to this pattern, the North Vietnamese and Pathet Lao forces launched offensives during the dry season (generally October to May), which were followed by ripostes during the wet season by RLG forces, with U.S. air support. This pattern seemed to follow an old Lao proverb, "When the water rises, the fish eat the ants. When the water falls, the ants eat the fish." The fighting during the first few years consisted largely of small-unit attacks on isolated positions, combat over road control points and tactical mountain-top sites in sparsely populated highland areas, ambushes, and hit-and-run encounters. The RLG retained control over the Mekong Valley regions, where the bulk of the lowland Lao live, and held certain adjacent mountain areas and a few scattered sites in enemy territory which they could reach only by aircraft. The Communist forces controlled the northern and eastern segments of the country, including all territory that borders on China and North Vietnam and the regions inhabited largely by highland minorities. Under the ground rules each side chipped at the other's holdings but neither seized substantial territory, even though forays were sometimes made (particularly by the FAR and its special guerrilla units) into enemy areas. This happened in 1966 with the FAR seizure of Nam Bac and in 1967 when FAR elements, moving into the PL heartland, reached the outskirts of Sam Neua town.[6]

A change in the pattern was evident by 1968 when both sides increased the intensity of their offensives. In March of that year the North Vietnamese launched a vigorous attack upon Phou Pha Thi, a secret U.S. radar station established in 1965 in Sam Neua Province, some seventeen miles from the North Vietnamese border. This station, operated by about a dozen U.S. technicians and guarded by some 100 Meo soldiers, was located on a mountain peak at an elevation of 8,000 to 9,000 feet, with an approach so steep on one side that it seemed almost impregnable to ground attack. Since the radar station was used to direct U.S. bombing missions over North Vietnam, the North Vietnamese were willing to take heavy losses as they overran the site on March 10.[7] The Communist campaign did not abate, as it had in previous years, with the onset of the rainy season. Instead, the NVA introduced eleven new battalions, according to U.S. estimates, many armed with effective Chinese AK-47 rifles (which were also supplied to some LPLA troops),[8] and the Communist gains were substantial, if not decisive. NVA and LPLA forces in Sam Neua Province cleared out most of the isolated RLG posts that had been supplied by air. In the north they drove off the Meo fighting forces defending Na Khang and in the south they forced the FAR forces to abandon Tha Theng. They also attacked certain Mekong Valley areas that previously had been seldom molested, assaulting an ordnance depot near Vientiane, ambushing several foreign aid teams working in villages, attacking Vientiane's airport, and crippling road traffic from time to time along the Mekong River road.

At the outset of the dry season, General Vang Pao, attempting a dramatic attack to compensate for the Communist gains, launched his Meo troops against enemy positions on the Plain of Jars. His forces, with U.S. air support, succeeded in levelling the provincial capital of Xieng Khouang and expelling the Communist troops. However, the success was only temporary, because several months later the Communist authorities again moved into the town.

Continuing to exert pressure during the wet season, the Communists launched an attack in June 1969 against RLG neutralist positions at Muong Suoi on the Plain of Jars. Two battalions of NVA, with Russian tanks and accompanied by LPLA units, overran the area and sent the RLG battalions in retreat. General Vang Pao's forces, with U.S. tactical air support, counterattacked and failed. Heavy losses were sustained in these engagements on both sides: an Associated Press account put governmental troops killed and wounded at 400, whereas the Communists (according to RLG sources) had 385 killed, largely by air bombardment.[9]

Fighting continued during the wet season and an RLG offensive, unequalled since the Geneva Conference of 1962, was launched in September 1969 against Communist positions on the Plain of Jars and in the Ho Chi Minh Trail area. Following an intensive American bombing operation, RLG assaults were made against a series of positions, including the towns of Xieng Khouang, Khang Khai, and Phong Savan on the Plain of Jars, Muong Phine in central Laos, and Tchepone further south in the Ho Chi Minh Trail area. The Communist forces were taken by surprise and fled their positions, abandoning huge stocks of arms and supplies.[10] General Vang Pao's forces then moved into positions on the Plain of Jars which had been held by Communist forces, at least since the 1962 Geneva Agreements. However, he had not held these positions many months before the NVA with LPLA participation launched a major offensive in February 1970, not only retaking their former positions on the Plain of Jars but expanding their territory as far as the RLG strongholds of Sam Thong and Long Tieng, which they attacked but did not succeed in holding. Some months later, following the U.S. incursion into Cambodia in May 1970, Communist forces seized the provincial capitals of Attopeu and Saravane, showing that they were interested in enlarging their stronghold in southern Laos in order to ensure the supply of their forces in South Vietnam and Cambodia following the loss of access to the port of Sihanoukville.

There was intense fighting throughout 1971 and 1972, intensifying in the latter part of the year and in 1973 in anticipation of a cease-fire that seemed likely to come in Laos, following the announced agreement between North Vietnam's chief negotiator in Paris, Le Duc Tho, and Henry Kissinger, the American principal negotiator. Although the pendulum pattern continued during these recent years, the Communists made substantial net gains. The most brutal fighting took place on and near the Plain of Jars, which both sides regarded as an area of strategic and symbolic importance. During the rainy season of 1971, an offensive by General Vang Pao's troops, preceded by heavy U.S. bombing, seized most of the Plain. As the dry season emerged, the road-bound communist forces, principally North Vietnamese, launched a massive attack in December, with tanks and long range guns and mortars, and in four days forced Vang Pao's forces off the Plain, seized Sam Thong and continued an assault against Long Tieng, where they were finally stopped. Heavy casualties resulted on both sides. Further devastating battles took place in the same area during 1972, with the Communist side emerging in early 1973 in control of most of the Plain. There was fighting elsewhere in Laos, although it did not exhibit the same ferocity as in the Plain of Jars area. In the southern panhandle region, the communists added to their segment of control, Thateng on the Bolovens Plateau and Paksong on the Plateau's northern entrance. In 1972, the NVA continued their steady advance from the Plateau toward Pakse. As on the Plain of Jars, the see-saw ground battles, accompanied by heavy U.S. bombing, increased the refugee flow largely in the direction of RLG-held territory and left a trail of obliterated towns in the south. For example, Saravane changed hands several times and was erased in the intermittent battles, remaining but a name on the map.

This brief description of recent military events shows that the standoff, by which both sides had remained principally in the areas of their control, with only small changes in territory, had been altered. The offensives conducted by the Communists, even during the dry season, and the bold advances of the RLG forces with increasing U.S. air bombardment and logistic assistance beginning in the fall of 1969, indicated a willingness by both sides to take larger military risks and to suffer commensurate damage to gain political advantage.

The most formidable weapon facing the Communist forces was U.S. airpower. While the RLG forces, with some notable exceptions, were generally a poor match for the NVA and their LPLA allies, the U.S. air engagements provided some measure of balance. The intensification of the ground war in 1969 was accompanied by a substantial increase in bombardment by U.S. planes. Air sorties in Laos, according to newspaper accounts, reached an average of about 12,500 a month during 1969 (compared with 4,700 sorties a month against targets in Laos and 12,000 sorties a month against North Vietnam at the time President Johnson called a halt to the bombing in 1968). American air operations appeared to have two missions: one (code-named Steel Tiger), largely with B-52s, was directed against NVA infiltration to South Vietnam; the other (called Barrel Roll), consisting of Phantoms and Thunderjets from Thailand and carrier-based bombers, was directed against NVA and LPLA in northern Laos.[11]

The havoc wreaked by the air war was painful to the inhabitants of the PL zone. Many NLHS governmental and military headquarters were located in caves. Fear of bombing forced residents to move into makeshift, underground shelters where some lived for months. The air bombardment accompanying the fall offensive against the towns on the Plain of Jars produced especially heavy damage, according to refugee reports. For example, in Phoung Savan, which was assaulted in September, refugees reported that there was not a house left standing.[12] This bombing, as well as the ground fighting, produced a sizable refugee flow from the embattled areas, apparently in both directions. However, flight to the RLG side, where there was no bombing (since the North Vietnamese have chosen not to employ their limited aircraft fleet in the war) was much greater than that to PL-controlled areas. Reports from RLG refugee officials in August 1969 stated that 80,000 refugees had already fled the northeastern provinces of Sam Neua and Xieng Khouang during the year.[13] In April 1970, according to testimony by an AID official before Senator Edward M. Kennedy's subcommittee on refugees, there were 246,000 refugees on the RLG side in Laos.[14] By the fall of 1972, there were approximately 300,000 refugees living in RLG camps.

Unquestionably the PL authorities are deeply concerned about the air bombardment.[15] Their radio broadcasts contain daily denunciations and they exert diplomatic pressure available to them to halt the bombing. Following the former Hanoi formula, they have tied future negotiations about Laos to a cessation of the bombing, stating that the U.S. "must halt their bombing raids on the zone of the patriotic forces so as to create conditions for the Laotians to settle among themselves their internal affairs, without U.S. interferences."[16] Nevertheless, they maintain publicly that they are able to cope with the air attacks. They intermittently proclaim a box score of the planes they have destroyed: on October 12, 1970, Pathet Lao radio announced that they had shot down over 1,500 U.S. planes since the start of the bombing.[17] Unofficial U.S. figures for plane losses in Laos during the same period, according to press reports, totaled about 400.

Military Structure

The PL fighting forces are divided into three principal categories: regular forces, regional (or popular) forces, and militia (or guerrilla) forces. Regular forces serve under the command of central, regional, or provincial commanders in battalion units or "independent" (ekalat) companies. Regional troops are generally drawn from the district or canton, and the militia from the canton or village. As in the Vietnamese Communist military structure, on which the PL military organization is modeled, troops may be recruited directly into the forces at any level, or they may graduate from a lower to higher echelon. The higher the echelon, generally the more competent the troops. The regular forces have the best training, equipment, and leadership, whereas the regional forces, as full-time troops, are generally more professional than the part-time, untrained, village soldiers.

Although press reports from Laos sometimes referred to "mixed" Vietnamese-Pathet Lao units, and to Vietnamese "encadrement" of PL forces, our data have not revealed the existence of any such combat units in the strict sense of these words. Regular battalions and companies of the Lao People's Liberation Army normally had a Vietnamese advisory team. Some of our interviewees spoke of small PL units, sometimes several squads, that served with Vietnamese units, largely as liaison agents, guides, porters, and auxiliary personnel who were useful because of their familiarity with local conditions. Several interviewees described some cases of Vietnamese and PL units designated by similar unit numbers and moving together in joint operations, although they ordinarily lived and operated separately.

The LPLA follows the same pattern of organization as that of the party, front, and government (see Figures 4-2 and 4-3). Central military headquarters is located at "the center" in Sam Neua, where Kaysone, who has served as the principal military leader since the 1940s, is in overall command. Reporting to

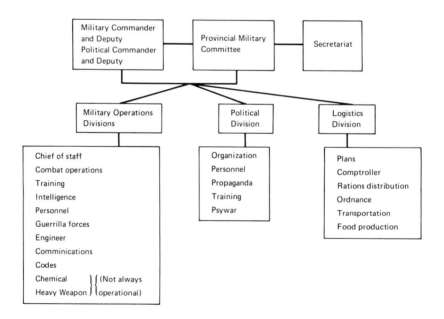

Figure 4-2. The Provincial Military Committee Structure

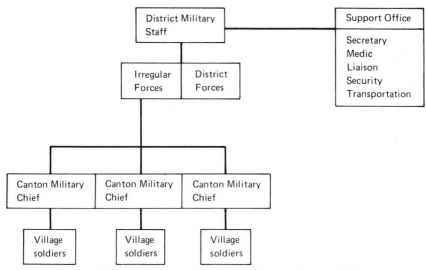

Figure 4-3. The Organization of District and Canton Military Forces

him is the LPLA Commander-in-Chief Major General Khamtay Siphandone. Subordinate to General Khamtay's supreme headquarters staff, which is served by a secretariat, is a military operations division, a political division, and a logistics division (see Figure 2-1).

Below the center, in the South Laos regional tactical headquarters commanded by General Phomma and in several regional headquarters are military headquarters at the province, district, canton, and village echelons. At each level the senior military commander is responsible for operations of all military forces and also serves as chief of the military affairs committee. This committee is subordinate to the party leadership.

The structure of the military organization of a southern province from which we have information is the same, with minor variations, as those in other provinces. The provincial military committee is composed of the provincial military and political commanders and their deputies. Serving them is a secretariat, which functions as the inspector general for the province and provides secretarial and communication services. (See Figure 4-2 for the organization of the provincial military committee.)

The district and canton are organized in much the same manner as the provincial military affairs committee. The district in the province described above had a force of some thirty full-time soldiers, charged with providing security for the district headquarters and for conducting limited operations in the immediate area. The canton military commander, a full-time soldier, was the chief of the canton's military affairs committee. He commanded six to eight soldiers in each village of the canton.

A relatively small number of "Patriotic Neutralist Forces," estimated at 2,725 in September 1969,[18] operate under the LPLA command. These are the forces of General Khammouane Boupha in Phong Saly and Colonel Deuane in Xieng Khouang, whose line of command is thought to run through Brigadier General Singkapo Chounramany, political chief of the Xieng Khouang regional headquarters.

Recruitment

Over the past twenty-five years, Pathet Lao cadres have used a blend of persuasion and coercion to recruit men to their forces. In the earlier years, they relied more heavily on persuasion, especially in the areas that they did not dominate. As the cadres established control, they could simply draft men into military service. However, even when they applied pressure, their doctrine required them to propagate the notion that their recruits had joined the revolutionary struggle of their own free will.

Several recruiting themes have persisted throughout PL history, principally the joint themes of anticolonialism and antiimperialism. From 1946 to 1954 they called upon their compatriots to expel the French colonialists; after 1954 their appeal was converted to the struggle against the American imperialists. The negative appeal to fight against the intruders was joined with the positive appeal to Lao patriotism—all Lao peoples must join in the struggle for independence. In addition, they appealed to self-interest, perhaps the most widely used offer being the promise of education to Lao youths, an opportunity that attracted parents and children alike.

Pathet Lao recruiters learned from their Viet Minh mentors that, although general themes were obviously to be used with all potential recruits, an effective recruiter must learn the living conditions and aspirations of his candidate and appeal to his desire for self-improvement. The recruiter also normally armed himself with the knowledge of how to apply the necessary pressure of coercion. The following excerpts from our interviews give an indication of the style and method of Pathet Lao recruitment.

A former Pathet Lao captain (A-20) summarized the recruitment process, showing both its persuasive and coercive aspects, in the following manner:

To recruit men for the army, they tell the people that Laos is a country rich in natural resources. It is a beautiful country, abundant in rivers and streams and great wealth. But the Lao people are still poor because of capitalism and U.S. imperialism. The young people—male and female—owners of Laos, regardless of race or tribe, must stand up, hand in hand in the struggle against U.S. imperialism.

Many people believe what they say. But some refuse to serve the Pathet Lao. The Pathet Lao say to them, "Why do you refuse when others volunteer? You should be patriotic. You should follow the majority." In other words, they threaten those who are reluctant to follow them.

Even though the anti-French feeling was not as virulent in Laos as in neighboring Vietnam, many Lao youths were caught up in the spirit of nationalism. Speaking of the climate of feeling among his friends in the early 1950s, one interviewee, (A-18) who was twenty years old at the time, said that he was "enthusiastic about independence. Everyone was talking about it." During this period PL recruiters were working closely with their Viet Minh advisers and had learned, as pointed out, the importance of tailoring their appeals to the personal situations of their candidates. This is the recruitment story of a former PL officer (A-21) who was a young student, attending the second grade in a village in southern Laos in 1952, and was recruited after he had failed an exam:

I had taken my final exam at Muong Mai, not far from my home village. I was disappointed because I had failed and went back to my home village. Just at that time a company of Pathet Lao, under the leadership of (later General) Phomma and Sithon Kommadam, were enjoying themselves, drinking and dancing in the village. I went to see them. General Phomma approached me and asked me about my exam. He knew I was disappointed because I had failed. So he suggested that I come with him, and I would be able to further my education. That seemed better to me than staying at home. It was enough to convince me. I went with him.

Though since a defector from the Pathet Lao ranks, he pointed out that he came to believe that he had enlisted in a just cause:

I believe the same as other young Lao. I was repeatedly told that Laos was a beautiful country, abundant in natural resources, but because of French colonialism the Lao people could not take advantage of their great wealth. Instead, the French had made the Lao people their slaves. The French had taken Lao resources and sent them to France. It was the duty of all young Lao to fight for the liberation of Laos. I firmly believed that at the time. I felt that I had to fight against the French imperialists.

In the early years of the PL movement, Viet Minh cadres not only worked hand-in-hand with Lao counterparts but also recruited directly among the population. The Vietnamese, too, found that a powerful appeal was the promise of an education, particularly a Vietnamese one. The following is the story of the recruitment of a young Lao (A-12) by Viet Minh cadres in 1954:

The Viet Minh called a meeting at night of all inhabitants of Muong Kao—even women and children—at the wat. There was entertainment, a play, and singing. The Vietnamese then made speeches. They asked parents if they wanted to send their children to study in Vietnam. They said that Vietnam was an advanced country, and that it offered a good opportunity for young Lao to gain knowledge. Many parents were convinced and asked that their children be selected. So the Vietnamese listed the names of the youths, maybe 200.

Like many others, this young man was not sent to school as he seems to have expected, but was given military training for the PL forces in North Vietnam.

However, in some cases young Lao were actually given an education and subsequently were required to perform military service. For example, an interviewee told us that he was one of thirty selected in his region to go to North Vietnam for education. Proving himself a good student, he was selected for medical studies, which he completed in North Vietnam, and later returned to serve as a doctor in a Pathet Lao military hospital in southern Laos.

The pattern of calling village meetings for purposes of recruitment was continued by Pathet Lao cadres after independence in 1954. A former PL soldier (A-6) told us he was recruited in 1959 by Singkhim, a son of Sithon Kommadam, who called a meeting in the village and said that "anyone who wanted to further his education should come with us." Another former PL soldier (A-8) provides an insight into how a promise of education combined with an implicit threat of coercion was used to take him into the army in 1960:

I was working on our farm. One day I was approached by a Pathet Lao recruiter who had come from Sam Neua. He promised to send me to Vietnam for study. At first I didn't want to leave my family, but then he told me that if I didn't go, they would draft me anyhow. So I went along. My family didn't want me to leave, but they couldn't do anything about it.

I only got as far as Sam Neua. There I was given a weapon and told that the situation in the country didn't allow them to send me to Vietnam now. I was told that I must first fight for my country. I was disappointed not to be able to study.

A story of recruitment following the rupture of relations between the Royal Lao Government and the Pathet Lao in 1959 came to us from a former PL soldier (A-12) who had been demobilized from the PL forces in 1958, when the integration agreement was pending, and was taken back into the PL forces the next year. Promoted to master sergeant and instructed to recruit thirty soldiers for his platoon, he gave a firsthand account of his methods. First he rounded up others who had been demobilized from the PL forces. In his words:

I said that the Second Pathet Lao Battalion had fled to the Plain of Jars and we need you to fight again. And I explained that Souphanouvong and others were imprisoned and it was impossible to unite with the other Lao. The only thing we could do was fight. Many believed me—they were angry with the government.

In addition to these former PL soldiers, he recruited other young men. He stated that he first requested them to join and noted that some volunteered. He added that "some refused, so I sent troops to surround their houses, then picked them up." Another former PL cadre, (A-13) also recruited in 1959, told a similar story. Three PL soldiers entered his village and told the nai ban (village chief) that they needed three young men. The nai ban said to him, "You have been selected to go with the PL. Go home and eat and get ready." "I ate and packed my things, while the three soldiers waited with the nai ban for me."

While many of the recruiting methods remained the same, after 1962, with the consolidation of Pathet Lao power in its zone and the development of a more rationalized army, the processes became more systematized. Describing the recruitment process in the region of Nam Tha, Captain Mai Dai Hap, former NVA adviser to a PL battalion, pointed out that the principal responsibility for recruitment lay at the district level with the popular troop command. The cadre in charge of popular troops had to canvas the villages, first establishing a list of youths eligible for military service and then sending out an appeal for volunteers. If the response was not adequate, a meeting with the people was organized by the cadres of the district military committee to discuss recruitment. The meetings were manipulated to give the appearance of being democratic, but the cadres applied great pressure on families to offer their sons for service. Quotas were set for each district, and if they were not reached by volunteers the men would be drafted. As pointed out above, there is a system for graduation of soldiers from one troop level to another, so that the needs of regional and main forces can also be served through this process.

Refugees from Xieng Khouang Province reported that the draft age was fifteen, but youngsters taken into service were often as young as twelve—which was also the case in the FAR—attesting to the growing exhaustion of human resources in Laos as a result of protracted war.[19] New conscripts appeared to have been assigned to the PL forces rather than to Deuanist units that were located in the province, making it appear that the Deuanists were declining as a viable force. Refugees also noted that parents often did not learn of a son's death until months after it occurred. The tax exemption of 100 kilos of rice for those who had a family member in the armed forces continued after death, but no other death benefits were conferred.[20]

Our data do not permit us to estimate the ethnic distribution of recruitment in the LPLA. From time to time, the Pathet Lao radio proclaimed the swelling of LPLA ranks with great numbers of volunteers from the diverse peoples of the "liberated" zone. For example, a broadcast on February 20, 1968, claimed that "in 1967, thousands of young men and women of various ethnic minorities volunteered to join" the regular and regional forces, increasing the total strength of the LPLA by 30 percent over that in 1966.[21] Mai Dai Hap (B-9), basing his judgment on his experience in the Nam Tha and Muong Sing regions and on discussions with other NVA advisers who attended a conclave at the northwest military region at Son La, North Vietnam, estimated that 60 to 70 percent of the LPLA were Lao Theung, and the rest were Lao Loum and other groups.

Although we cannot estimate the extent to which women served in the PL military forces, we did note intermittent mention of their role by Pathet Lao Radio. For example, a broadcast of April 24, 1967, stated that "during the first three months of this year, 100 young women volunteered for the army in Southern Laos ... in Sam Neua, already 40 women enrolled in the LPLA."[22] A broadcast in June 1967 noted that Xieng Khouang Province "now has its own women guerrilla platoons and squads."[23] Another broadcast in October 1968 speaks of "militia women" who "fought the enemy with the very weapons they had captured from them."[24] In the NLHS pamphlet, *Phoukout Stronghold*, there is a story of Xinma, a Meo guerrilla leader whose leadership ability led to her promotion "as a political commissar of her village militia," and there is mention of "six women of the militia-platoon of village X" who "put ten enemy troops out of action."[25]

We should mention here the LPLA campaign to promote defections and surrenders among the enemy forces, even though it was designed more to demoralize the enemy than it was to recruit PL soldiers. Company political officers were charged with conducting campaigns to promote enemy defections and surrenders consistent with local conditions, and specialized units were assigned to conduct more elaborate programs such as radio broadcasts and propaganda leaflet distribution. For example, a leaflet we examined contained the appeal of a former royal army soldier, now serving with the PL, to his former comrades to join the true "defenders of the Lao people." The leaflet promised that defectors "will be welcomed and given a responsible job and security." On the other hand, if they continue to work with the American imperialists, they will be "wiped out with them." Company officers were given explicit instructions for dealing with prisoners, as revealed in a radio broadcast that was part of a weekly series devoted to company political work:

We must know what they are thinking, know if they are afraid of us or not, so we can formulate plans and slogans to encourage disbanded soldiers to surrender quickly. At the same time, political cadres must remind and guide their own companies to definitely and correctly implement the Neo Lao Hak Sat central command's policies toward the enemy who are captured or surrender. They must never be beaten, held in contempt, threatened, or have their personal belongings taken away. Naturally, however, all POW's must be disarmed and all their documents taken away. Those prisoners who are stubborn, oppose our policy and lines, or oppose our cadres and soldiers, who have treated them fairly, must be punished.

Afterward, we must pay special attention to explaining to the prisoners the central command's correct and just amnesty policy and the importance of getting rid of stubborn reactionary soldiers who committed crimes against the people.[26]

A PL document (MK-1) providing guidance for dealing with prisoners shows that captured enemy soldiers were given political indoctrination aimed at showing them the crimes of the governmental side and the justice of the PL struggle. Those who were thought to have learned their "lessons" and seem reliable were taken into the PL forces. The LPLA sources made regular claims about enemy defectors. For example, a Pathet Lao News Agency release on April 20, 1968, claimed that more than 2,100 troops of the "puppet army" had defected, deserted, or surrendered during the preceding five months of the dry season (November to March), a number equivalent to those who had abandoned their ranks during the first ten months of the previous year.[27] We do not have sufficient data to assess these specific claims, yet it is clear that both the LPLA and the FAR have, over the years, added defectors to their ranks.

Training

The vast majority of recruits who joined the Lao People's Liberation Army were young peasants with unformed political ideas, little education, and no military skills. The aim of training was to inculcate attitudes, habits, and skills that produce an effective Lao Communist soldier. There were three strands to the LPLA effort: political indoctrination; basic education, or "cultural studies," as they were officially called; and military training. In all three strands, the regular forces received considerably more training then the regional forces which, in turn, were more exposed to training than the guerrilla forces.

Military Training

Training in discipline, fighting skills, and other military subjects was given within the soldier's unit, at special schools in Laos such as the Kommandam Officers School in Sam Neua Province, at the noncom schools in each PL province, and at medical and other specialized training programs, as well as in North Vietnnam. Each training program developed a specialized curriculum, yet all soldiers generally received instruction in the fighting techniques one would find in a rudimentary ground combat force.

Former NVA Captain Mai Dai Hap (B-9) stated that the training program for the Lao soldiers in the battalion he advised included the "five great techniques": creeping and crawling, digging fortifications, firing a rifle, fighting with bayonet, and use of a grenade. Instruction was given in various tactics: methods of ambush, hand-to-hand combat, breaching perimeter defenses, and similar topics. As air power had grown as a major threat, training stressed protection of personnel and methods of firing against aircraft. Lectures were given on health, with attempts to abolish such superstitious practices as animal sacrifice for driving away sickness and to inculcate concepts of proper sanitation.

Basic Education

The LPLA is one of the primary agents for providing a rudimentary education in the PL zone. Illiteracy is widespread within the LPLA ranks. Mai Dai Hap (B-9) estimated that most of the squad and platoon leaders in his PL battalion could not read or write, and that the company- and battalion-level officers could read only a little. Although learning to read and write Lao may be difficult even for a

Lao Loum soldier, it is a task even more difficult for an uneducated Lao Theung or Meo soldier whose knowledge of the Lao language is rudimentary.

The LPLA participates in the general NLHS campaign to teach the reading and writing of Lao, a program that has no FAR counterpart. An official slogan states that "a person who knows only one word shall teach a person who knows none; a person who knows two words shall teach a person who knows only one . . . ." We do not have the information to judge the success of this campaign.

For a great majority of the troops, the literacy training in the army was the only formal schooling to which they were exposed. Some interviewees who attended training schools reported that those who could not read or write were first given literacy training, and instruction was sometimes offered in other subjects such as arithmetic and geography. The pamphlets used in this basic education included simple stories with clear political messages. One, for example, entitled "If I Must Die, You Will Also Die," is the story of an LPLA soldier who has fought to the end and, in a final effort before dying, throws a grenade at the enemy and shouts "Death to the American imperialists and their lackeys." Another, "A New Recruit Kills the Aggressor," tells the story of a young Lao soldier who fights hand-to-hand against an American officer who commands a convoy of arms on Route 13. Still another shows several situations in which PL soldiers protect the local inhabitants from barbaric U.S. soldiers.

Political Training

Following the model of their North Vietnamese mentors, who in turn were greatly influenced by the Chinese Communists, LPLA leaders regard political indoctrination to be even more important than the transmission of military skills. They believed that the principal source of their military strength was "fighting will." While they conceded an asset of the enemy was his superior technology and firepower, especially his massive air strength, they asserted that "as long as we grasp the spirit of heroism we can defeat the enemy."[28] Indeed, in 1969, the LPLA leadership asserted that victory was near. However, they recognized that "the nearer we approach complete victory, the fiercer the fighting."[29]

Since fighting will is the key to victory, soldiers must be inculcated with proper revolutionary thoughts. The lessons are simple and frequently repeated, teaching the soldier who his enemy is and why he is fighting. They are often given in the form of questions and answers, which the soldier must memorize, and are sometimes transmitted by cadres reading to small groups from printed training materials.

Some excerpts from a widely used training document (LP-9) portray the style and content of political indoctrination:

Laos is abundant with natural resources—what makes the Lao people suffer scarcity?

Laos has a vast land for cultivation and forests that are abundant with all kinds of timber and wild animals. Other natural resources are also plentiful. However, the Lao people are not able to make use of these resources because of the aggression and oppression of foreign countries, in particular the French colonialists and American imperialists.

What is revolution? Why should we be engaged in the struggle for revolution?

Naturally, everybody wants to be happy and to live a better life. But we can never be happy so long as we have vampires—the American imperialists and their lackeys—sucking our blood. Revolution is the only way to wipe out this condition. So we have no choice but to fight to free ourselves from oppression, and to build a new society that will offer a better life and happiness.

Instructions to cadres for indoctrination of the troops contain simple lessons for inculcating revolutionary behavior but rarely mention Marxism or Leninism. Political cadres are admonished to pay special attention to a newspaper published by the LPLA (in English, *The Liberation Army*),[30] as well as to "reports released by the armed forces, local news and daily news broadcasts by Radio PL to keep cadres and fighters informed."[31]

It is clear from the excerpts above, as well as from the earlier discussion of recruitment, that the primary theme of political indoctrination has been the oppression of Laos by foreign colonialists and imperialists. They are blamed for that backwardness of the country, for the "feudalism and subjugation" that exists in those areas which have not been "liberated." The Lao people are capable of development, but they have been retarded by intruders. For example, an LPLA leader in Muong Sai (LP-3), commemorating the twenty-first anniversary of the LPLA, on January 20, 1967, said that "the Lao people are hardworking and courageous, full of strength and intelligence, with good will, wishing only peace and independence for their country," that the causes of the war and unhappiness are not an ill-fated destiny, "as many old people frequently say," but are "due to the intervention of the American and other imperialists like the French." LPLA doctrine, in Maoist style, also claims that the armed forces are fighting a "people's war," and are "wholeheartedly serving the nation and the people, and are correctly carrying out the mass line."[32]

In the manner of Mao Tse-tung and Vo Nguyen Giap, the LPLA political instruction stresses certain rules of proper behavior. These, too, are simple and frequently repeated. A calendar published by the LPLA propaganda and training section in 1966 lists eight rules and eight oaths of the LPLA as well as "twelve rules for dealing with people," meant for memorization, all designed to encourage revolutionary consciousness, self-discipline, and correct behavior toward civilians.[33]

Great emphasis during political training is placed on the need for "tightening the bonds between the armed forces and various ethnic groups." Soldiers are told that even though the LPLA is composed of various tribes and ethnic groups and members are from different provinces and localities, they make up a single unified, national force serving in a common cause to liberate their country from the intrusion of American imperialists and their hirelings. All LPLA troops are instructed to show proper respect and appreciation for the customs and traditions of various minorities. The following guidance to cadres was found in a training document (LBN-3):

> Strive to eliminate conflict among the tribes.
> Recruit tribal people into the armed forces.
> Safeguard the traditions of the tribes and show respect
>   for their chiefs.
> Give medical care to tribal peoples.
> Enlighten tribal peoples about our struggle, and teach
>   them who are their friends and enemies.

The Lao People's Liberation Army uses a variety of organizational techniques, most modeled on the NVA and often related to Chinese Communist methods, for the inculcation of their political lessons. The LPLA has adopted the political commissar system, employing a dual set of officers reaching down as far as the company level, with one line responsible for military affairs and the other, probably more powerful, responsible for political affairs. The duty of providing political indoctrination falls to the political officer, with the company level being the focus. To influence the "thoughts and political outlook" of the troops, the political officer is instructed to be aware of their moods and know their routine. He should understand their problems and accompany them in combat to share their fears.

Another organizational technique serving to reinforce political training, adopted from the NVA, is the use of criticism and self-criticism meetings. Like the criticism ritual in the NVA, there is a wide variety of uses of these meetings, including sessions to review behavior, examine questions of discipline, discuss performance of work, mold fighting spirit, and scrutinize proper revolutionary thinking. One interviewee (A-20) described the series of criticism sessions that were held in his battalion, a practice followed with variations by other units. Their three-man cell held a daily session to discuss behavior; the squad met every three days to review behavior; the platoon held weekly sessions with a political cadre posing questions; company sessions each month were directed by the company political officer; and the battalion might meet every six months. At the company session, the political officer examined seven items: military discipline; unity with the people; work performance of the units; accomplishments; means of self- and group improvements; identification of outstanding persons; and plans for future activities.

While the LPLA criticism techniques are modeled upon those of the NVA, they are obviously altered to conform to the Lao cultural context. Revealing his

North Vietnamese bias, Mai Dai Hap (B-9) expressed a certain contempt for the PL criticism sessions, contending that the Lao did not know how to speak at a meeting, had difficulty distinguishing fact from fancy, and had a curious sense of personal honor—if a soldier were to say that he was leaving for home, he might simply be mildly reprimanded by an officer, whereas in the NVA such behavior would be regarded as a serious offense. These criticism sessions might appear freewheeling and lax to an NVA officer, accustomed to the practices in the royal Lao army, yet they would be judged severe and rigorous by an RLG officer.

A 1967 NLHS pamphlet, *Phoukout Stronghold*, which glorifies PL heroism in battle, noted that Phoukout units had "pushed forward the 'three-wells' drive: fight well, produce well and discharge every responsibility well."[34] This "three-wells" campaign followed North Vietnamese and Chinese Communist practice in building combat morale. A series of broadcasts during the latter half of 1969 revealed that political officers were instructed to organize a new program of special cadres, known as "unit thirty-three personnel" who were to take leadership in political indoctrination and morale-building activities. The unit thirty-three cadres were assigned to "review routine work habits, help clarify questions concerning the troops' way of thinking, fighting, and working spirit, and were to set a good example for others."[35] It is the duty of the political officer to maintain constant contact with the unit thirty-three at all levels, to learn of current conditions from them, and to instruct them "to praise the virtues of the troops, correct their mistakes, and help them promote their ideals."[36]

Another special campaign apparently launched during the summer of 1968 recognized "three-good fighters" and "three-good companies." This is an emulation program, modeled on the NVA as well as Chinese Communist practice,[37] singling out individual and unit models for awards. The goals are to "fight well, carry out good political work, ensure food production and observe thrift."[38] For example, a PL radio broadcast described a Houa Phan provincial meeting during July 1969, attended by 105 "three-good fighters" from guerrilla, regional, and regular forces, as well as local dignitaries, where the qualities of the soldiers were lauded and medals were distributed to them. Subsequent broadcasts urged units that had not yet named their three-good companies to do so, and made it appear that this was a zonewide campaign. On October 4, 1970, the Plain of Jars-Xieng Khouang military sector held its second "Three-Good Congress" attended by high-ranking military and political figures, including Kaysone, who addressed the meeting and awarded medals.[39]

We cannot judge the extent to which the political indoctrination is internalized. However, our discussions with defectors suggest that most soldiers believe what they are told. The majority have a low level of political sophistication; the lessons are not challenged by other sources of information and they seem generally not to be contradicted by personal experience. Testimony from a former PL cadre (A-2) reinforces this impression:

Most of the men recruited by the Pathet Lao are from poor families. They are taught repeatedly about the injustices of the government. They say to these people, "Do you know why your families are poor, and why you can't go to school?" The answer is, "The government doesn't care about your families. There is no school in your village and no hospital. The only way to improve your life is to overturn the government and drive out the enemy [they mean the Americans]. Once the government has been overthrown, and all the Americans are driven out, then we can work together for the improvement of our family and our country."

Most of those who are taught these lessons believe them. They come from poor families and when promised a brighter future they seem happy about it. . . . Of course, there may be a few who don't believe them.

While there is little apparent reason, or opportunity, for the LPLA soldier to challenge the political lessons, the extent of his internalization of the political ideas depends, to an important extent, upon the intensity and duration of his exposure to this training.

On the question of harmony between the ethnic groups, our limited sample permits us only an impressionistic account. One interviewee (A-20), whose unit contained both Lao Loum and Lao Theung, claimed that there were no ethnic problems, "since the men had been trained that there must be unity." While this response obviously simplifies a complicated issue, his attitude was shared by several other interviewees. We were interested that a number of our Lao Loum interviewees spoke of the Lao Theung as better fighters than the Lao Loum, leading us to wonder whether there is a stereotype, perhaps based upon fact, about the superior fighting qualities of the highlanders. For several interviewees, Lao Theung poverty made them a special target for Pathet Lao recruiters and, for unexplained cultural reasons, they were thought to enjoy fighting. One interviewee (A-3) put it this way:

The Kha like to fight. Many are killed, but they still continue to fight. They are different from the Lao. When there was no order to fight, they looked sad. They were never afraid of death.

Several interviewees (A-3, A-20, A-21, A-25) shared the view, stated by a former LPLA cadre in southern Laos, that the "Kha are braver fighters than the Lao Loum." Asked how he differed his political instruction between Lao Loum and Lao Theung troops, this officer (A-21) replied:

I emphasized different topics when I spoke to the Kha. The Kha tribesmen are very poor, living in the mountains without enough food or clothes. I told them we wanted to give them a better life. But I never gave them better expectation about promotion. When I spoke to the Lao, I talked about promotion.

To conclude this discussion of political training, we once again emphasize the importance of the LPLA as a socializing agency within the Lao Patriotic Front system. Young men, and a certain number of women, are recruited into the armed forces with little knowledge of their country and few political notions. Having grown up in a restricted milieu that emphasizes separateness, their world revolves around their own ethnic group or tribe, those who speak their language or come from their region. Drawn into a relatively disciplined military organization, they are indoctrinated with a new conception of their country, pressure is applied on them to work with diverse peoples, their political friends and enemies are defined for them, and the cause for which they fight is identified. Helped by the image of an outside enemy, the American imperialist, they are urged toward the sense of a national identity as Lao citizens. Taken from a kinship group or tribe whose habits and values are determined by tradition, they are instructed to conform to the rules of a relatively modern military organization. Some learn to read and write, some acquire a new language, and all develop certain military skills. We do not have the means to measure the total impact of this training, or indeed of the entire military experience, yet we are convinced that the PL soldier undergoes a significant change that will, in turn, affect the larger society in which he lives.

Aspects of the Military Life and Career

Since our limited number of interviews with former soldiers covered a diversity of experience and periods of sacrifice, our picture of their military life and career is impressionistic. Therefore, we present the following discussion tentatively, not in the sense that it represents a description of the life of a typical soldier but in an attempt to convey some sense of the quality of life that some soldiers, if only a few, have described.

Even within the Lao context, the LPLA soldier receives little remuneration. A former second lieutenant (A-3) told us that he received 200 grams of salted fish and 20 grams of salt daily, plus a subsistence payment (he said it was not a salary) of 500 kip monthly (500 kip equals approximately one dollar). Another soldier (A-1) stated that in his unit a private was paid 300 kip, a corporal to sergeant 400 kip, a staff sergeant to master sergeant 450 kip, a second lieutenant to captain 500 kip, and higher officers 700 kip monthly. Still another lieutenant (A-13) reported that he was paid 500 kip a month, in addition to his food. To give some sense of the buying power of his meager allowance, he said that in the town of Ban Ban he could by an egg for 5 kip and a chicken for 300 kip. A Japanese transistor radio cost from 40,000 to 60,000 kip.

It appears that a green fatigue uniform and basic food rations were generally provided to soldiers in regular units, and that they supplemented their food, when possible, by trading with villagers with the little money, salt, and other provisions they were given. Soldiers whose units were stationary, and whose tasks permitted, sometimes grew vegetables and raised pigs to improve their diet. A soldier who served in the quartermaster section of his unit said that 700 grams of rice per day per soldier was provided to the unit cook. A soldier's average meal consisted of rice, salt, canned or dried fish, and supplements provided from time to time by the soldier himself or the unit mess.

We gained the impression that the officer-enlisted men relationship is relatively equalitarian. Officers seem to share the same conditions as the men, eating the same food and sleeping where the men sleep. The officers' subsistence allowance is slightly larger than the men's, as we have indicated, but all allowances are so small that the remuneration makes little difference in their style of life. Officers' uniforms do not carry rank insignia and, according to one interviewee (A-13), all officers, regardless of rank, were addressed (at least in his unit) as *Phou Kong*, meaning chief.

Several indicators suggest to us that class background is a consideration for promotion. A captured personal history form (SAV-1) shows that a series of questions is posed to the soldier regarding his own class background and those of his family and his wife's family. He is queried whether anyone in his own or his wife's family has ever worked for "the imperialists" or for the government. A former PL cadre (A-31) whose family had been classed as petit bourgeois (naithun no) confirmed this impression, at least in his own case, when asked whether his family's qualification affected his career:

Of course it affected me. When I first joined them, I was not trusted until long afterwards. I tried to improve myself. I volunteered to do hard jobs that other people did not want to do. Afterwards, they praised me. They said that Naithun No can be improved and can be even better than other classes.

It appears that upper-class status tends to be an initial liability for advancement in the LPLA, though it does not necessarily preclude mobility within the officer ranks.

Our interviews gave some sense of the kinds of misbehavior that crop up in the ranks of the LPLA. Excessive drinking, smoking opium, gambling, and flirting with the girls were mentioned frequently as minor infractions. A more serious infraction that was apparently not uncommon was violation of the prohibition against marriage before the age of thirty by LPLA soldiers. Crimes that occurred intermittently were disobedience to officers, absence without leave, mistreatment of civilians, and cowardice in battle. There were some cases, too, of serious personal crimes such as robbery, rape, and murder.

A variety of punishments were used to fit the crimes. Just as the criticism session is important in training, it is the primary mechanism for maintaining control and discipline. Generally, the more serious the infraction, the higher the unit level of the criticism meeting. At some meetings, the violator is required to subject himself to self-examination and hear the criticism of both his peers and his superiors, and is assigned a program of self-study and self-improvement. The shame of public criticism and the group pressure to conform are frequently sufficient incentive to turn the soldier to the proper path. If his misbehavior is repetitive, other punishment may be given.

One soldier (A-31) described a punishment adopted by his commanding officer when soldiers continued to disobey instructions:

He made them lie down inside a mosquito net all day. They were not allowed to get up, except to go to the latrine. They were given only rice soup, and they had to lie down even while eating. He gave them a notebook and told them to write down everything they had done to violate regulations. Some of them would be in this position from three to seven days.

Though this sort of punishment is unusual, it suggests a variation available to commanders. Several interviewees spoke of jail sentences for soldiers who had committed serious crimes. One defector claimed that a soldier in his unit who violated the marriage rule would be separated from his wife for at least a year, and he would be subjected to three or four months' imprisonment. Another stated that in his unit the penalty would be two months' detention.

As in other armies, there is a system of individual and group rewards and incentives to encourage desired behavior. There is a hierarchy of medals and citations, and the LPLA command and central committees of the NLHS are frequently quoted by PL radio as having distributed first-class freedom medals, second-class medals, liberation third-class medals, emulation banners, and a variety of others. These awards are often given during ceremonies commemorating special holidays or events when important personalities may confer the title of "Iron Fighter," with speeches lauding the soldier's behavior as worthy of emulation.[40]

Concluding Comments

As in other underdeveloped societies, the Lao People's Liberation Army derives its strength in part from the fact that it is a disciplined organization in a little-organized society. The North Vietnamese have worked vigorously in developing the LPLA, assisting in recruitment and training, financing, supplying of weapons, ammunition, and equipment, selection and schooling of officers, and providing guidance in strategy and tactics. It is in large measure due to this Vietnamese guidance and support that the LPLA has reached its present level of effectiveness.

The LPLA performs a variety of functions. Most important, along with the NVA it has fought the war. In recruiting, training, and organizing its members to carry out this task it acts as a socializing agent, seeking to impart new values, attitudes, and habits. In addition, the LPLA is a primary instrument of the Lao Communist system of administration, persuasion, and control throughout the Pathet Lao zone. It also performs an important economic role, contributing to agricultural production, civic action projects, reconstruction of war damage, road-building, transportation, and communication.

The Lao, judged by the performance of both the Royal Lao Government and

PL armies, do not have an impressive military aptitude, when compared with their neighbors. We cannot measure empirically the capability of each side to deal with the other alone, since both have enjoyed significant external support. However, we can note that the Forces Armées Royales with American supplies, are much better equipped than the LPLA, who depend largely upon the North Vietnamese to outfit them. The FAR outclass the LPLA in firepower, mobility, technical equipment and clothing, indeed in almost all material ways. The LPLA, on the other hand, seem to have a more effective organization, better leadership, especially at the middle and lower levels, and a stronger will to fight.

The techniques of military organization, which are the great source of strength of the Vietnamese Communists, have been adopted by the LPLA. Though these techniques have not been as effective in Laos, they have been important to the LPLA. Party cadres within the military structure transmit party policy, keep alive the "revolutionary consciousness" of the troops, serve as model soldiers, and act as an intelligence network for the leadership. Political officers, as in the NVA (as well as in the Communist Chinese and Soviet armies), play an important role in maintaining morale and inspiring commitment on the part of the troops. Self-criticism sessions, as in other Communist armies, are a key instrument for maintaining discipline, developing group spirit, assessing strengths and weaknesses, and generally in guiding group behavior. Each of these control mechanisms, and others, have developed the strength and cohesion of the LPLA.

5 Concluding Observations

The aim of this chapter is to point up certain salient features of Pathet Lao leadership and organization and, especially, to note important gaps in our knowledge.

We have described the social and cultural context in which the Lao Communist movement has been nurtured. Within this context, the party, the army, and the front—the familiar Communist "tripod"—have been established as the principal institutions, and the leaders who dominate them, with the guidance of their North Vietnamese allies, wield the power. However, political patterns of traditional Laos still persist, and combine with the new Communist forms. For example, some of the PL leaders have accumulated their authority primarily as members of the important families of lowland Laos or as chieftains of tribal minorities in the highlands, deriving their power as much from ascriptive sources as from the Communist institutions they have established.

Although we have been able to identify what appears to be the most influential group of PL leaders, we cannot with confidence rank individuals in order of importance. There are indications that, as secretary-general of the party and minister of defense, Kaysone is the principal figure and that his deputy in the party, Nouhak, may be second in command. Prince Souphanouvong, chairman of the NLHS, or Lao Patriotic Front, is presented to the public, both within Laos and internationally, as the leading NLHS spokesman, but his decision-making power seems to be less than that of Kaysone and Nouhak. Souphanouvong is given greater public prominence than Kaysone and Nouhak, yet we have not noted an attempt to build a cult of personality, as in the days of Stalin, or to create the adulation enjoyed by Mao Tse-tung or Ho Chi Minh. Although Souphanouvong may not have power equivalent to that of Kaysone and Nouhak, it does not seem likely that, as some analysts contend, he is simply a figurehead manipulated by the Communist movement because of his aristo-cratic origins and personal appeal in Laos and abroad. Rather, his popularity within Laos, his strong personal qualities of leadership, and his long-standing prominence in the movement make it probable that he does still wield significant influence.

Any question regarding the relative power of any Lao Communist leaders must be put in the context of another question—the role of the North Vietnamese in the Lao Communist decision-making process. We know that the North Vietnamese have played a decisive role in the founding, growth, and persistence of the Pathet Lao's organization. We know that they continue to play a critical military and political role, with some 50,000 to 67,000 troops serving in the country and a network of advisers placed throughout the most important PL institutions. There is little question that the North Vietnamese exercise critical influence on PL decisions, yet we do not have an insider's view of the decision-making process. Obviously, the crucial decisions affecting North Vietnamese troop deployment, strategy, and tactics were made by the North Vietnamese. When matters were more clearly identified as being within Lao Communist jurisdiction, it appears that the North Vietnamese worked through the Lao leadership, with relative sensitivity to their nationalist sensibilities. However, we do not know which leaders the North Vietnamese may have consistently favored or which they may have distrusted. We have not been able to follow the possible fluctuations in the relationship of the North Vietnamese to the Pathet Lao, although as the North Vietnamese military investment increased in recent years and the war escalated it seems likely that North Vietnamese influence in the PL decision-making process correspondingly increased.

Although we have noted the cohesion and stability of the PL leadership, we have not been able to identify the cliques and factions that are likely to be present in this as they are in other Communist systems. There were a number of important issues that might have provided a source of factional alignments, as has been the case in North Vietnam and China. Was there a difference of opinion regarding the pace and scope of the war, as there seems to have been in North Vietnam? Did some leaders prefer to reduce the military conflict in favor of a political offensive, possibly offering temporary accommodation with the RLG? Were there differences on the question of alignment in the Sino-Soviet dispute? Most importantly, were there differences concerning the PL relationship with the North Vietnamese? The answer to this last, critical question may be the key to many of the other questions that could be posed, and it requires further discussion.

It is reasonable to assume that the worldwide trend within national Communist parties toward diversity and autonomy has influenced the thinking of certain Lao Communist leaders. Moreover, dependence upon the Vietnamese runs against the Lao historical grain. It should be recalled that the original split of the PL wing from the Lao Issara in 1949 concerned the issue of cooperation with the Viet Minh (an issue that still divides the PL and the Royal Lao Government today). Some PL leaders, as Lao nationalists, must entertain misgivings about their heavy dependence upon their traditional enemy, even when—perhaps especially when—they receive scarce resources and valuable advice. Some of the PL leaders must be pondering the painful question, do Lao interests always coincide with those of the Vietnamese, whose decisions must be based first upon their own national interests and purposes. Indeed, some PL leaders might well believe that the intensity of the war on Lao soil was a product of their intimate involvement with the Vietnamese. On the other hand, the Lao

Communist leaders have developed a habit of dependency upon the Vietnamese and must feel that they share common interests and a beneficial partnership. Further, since their RLG opponents receive massive support from the Americans and, to a lesser degree, the Thais, PL leaders must recognize that their small and relatively weak movement badly needs external assistance. These latter factors make it likely that PL leaders will continue to lean heavily upon their North Vietnamese neighbors. Indeed, it is possible that, in view of the deep North Vietnamese involvement in their system, they have no other feasible choice.

Another question about which we can only speculate concerns how the next generation of PL leaders will differ from the current one. It seems likely that if the current PL-RLG separation continues, more future PL leaders will come from the ethnic minorities. Highland tribes populate roughly 80 percent of the PL-controlled zone, where a campaign of recruitment for education and party membership, selecting the brightest and most ambitious youths, has been under way for nearly a decade. Lao Theung already comprise 60 percent of the party membership, according to the North Vietnamese economic cadre we have cited. As younger cadres return from their studies in North Vietnam, China, the Soviet Union, and other Communist countries, what changes will they bring to the leadership? With more technical education and a stronger formal dose of Marxism-Leninism than the present incumbents, how will their policy inclinations differ from those of the present leaders? What will be the nature of their nationalism? How committed are they likely to be to reunification with the lowland areas of Laos? From an RLG perspective, it is likely that an anti-Communist Lao Loum elite will be even less enthusiastic about sharing power with Marxist-Leninist ethnic minority leaders than with the current, predominantly Lao Loum, PL leadership, which includes relatives, former classmates, and associates in government.

Because of limited information it is extremely difficult to assess public attitudes toward PL authority. However, it is clear that these attitudes were shaped by a life of hazard and severe hardship. American bombing of selected areas of the PL zone has been the heaviest in world history, and thousands have fled to the RLG areas to escape it. In some areas inhabitants spent their daylight hours in damp caves or underground dugouts, emerging only at night to conduct their necessary activities. Devastation has been enormous, and the burdens placed upon those who remained have been heavy. Most able-bodied men, and some women, have been conscripted into military service; tax levies were high; the requirements of porterage and other corvée labor were onerous.

This tragic picture of life in the PL zone is clear, but the political attitudes of the population are not. Refugees, who may wish to appear friendly to the RLG authorities, often stress the oppressive aspects of PL rule, especially the heavy work assignments, monotonous political propaganda, limitations on personal movement, heavy taxes, and interference by Vietnamese advisers. However, there is reason to believe that those who have stayed, and perhaps some who have fled, respect and are committed to the PL authorities—an attitude similar to that of the North Vietnamese population toward their leaders. A majority of the remaining families have sons serving with the PL military forces, giving them a strong personal investment in the PL cause. In addition, the bombing and other hostilities may have created a feeling that people must rally around their leaders and fight against the power that seems bent on bombing them to capitulation.

Another factor in the assessment of public attitudes in the PL zone was the popular feeling toward the presence of North Vietnamese troops and advisers. The North Vietnamese made significant efforts to maintain a low profile within Laos. They endeavored to post their troops out of the population centers and have generally refrained from making onerous direct demands upon the local population. The advisers, who were normally adept at learning the local language and customs and living at the level of their hosts, made a strong effort, in the words of several refugees, to "not let themselves be seen." Even though these measures seem to have succeeded in reducing popular resentment, we have the impression that a certain amount of popular antipathy toward the active North Vietnamese role in Laos remained.

The impact of the war and the flight of the refugees raise a series of questions that we can pose but not answer. Almost one half of the population of the current PL-controlled area has fled to RLG territory during the past decade. How severely has the drain of population affected the PL authorities and the remaining population? What was the effect of continued bombing and warfare on those who stayed. Looking ahead to happier prospects of peace, how many and which refugees are likely to return to their home territories?

We have pointed out at numerous stages of this study that present PL capacity—political, administrative, and military—was attributable, in good part, to North Vietnamese guidance and assistance. An interesting question is what would have happened if this support had been seriously diminished or removed. As for the administrative and political institutions, their competence would surely have declined. But, since it is not clear how firmly these institutions had taken root in Lao soil, it is not evident whether the loss would have been disastrous or merely serious. Speculating about the effect on the Pathet Lao military capacity following the removal of North Vietnamese assistance is even more difficult. It seems likely that if the Royal Lao Government had maintained its external support from the Thais and the United States, including the massive bombing, while the Lao People's Liberation Army was stripped of North Vietnamese assistance, the LPLA could have been routed. But the reverse is even more likely—that is, if external assistance had been stripped from the RLG, while the NVA support to the LPLA remained constant, the Forces Armées Royales could easily have been overrun. There is no empirical way of measuring a third possibility—how the LPLA would have fared against the FAR if neither had outside support. Certainly the volume of violence would have declined if the more powerful outsiders departed.

As a new phase in Lao history is introduced with the cease-fire agreement of early 1973, it seems likely that the level of external intervention within Laos will decline, but foreign powers will undoubtedly continue to exert an important influence upon internal Lao politics. Our study concludes that the Pathet Lao movement, having grown in the past two decades from a small insurgent organization to a counter-government dominating more than two thirds of the territory and one third of the population will be a powerful competitor in the struggle for political domination of Laos.

Appendixes

Appendix A: Background and Profiles of Pathet Lao Leaders

Origins of the Pathet Lao Leadership, 1945-49[a]

In the early years of the Lao independence movement, following the defeat of Japan and the reestablishment of French power, the Lao who later founded what was to be known as the Pathet Lao operated in two principal areas. One stretched from the eastern regions of Laos across the border to northwestern Vietnam where bands of Lao guerrillas were organized with the active assistance of the Viet Minh. The other was in Thailand, where a number of future Pathet Lao leaders had fled to participate in the Lao Issara government-in-exile. These two areas of operation had a great deal of interaction, partly due to the fact that Vietnamese funds went into the support of the Lao independence movement, both in Bangkok and in eastern Laos. Small guerrilla bands throughout Laos often had liaison with both centers (though sometimes with neither) and group leaders frequently traveled to each other's territory. In this early period, rather than drawing clear political lines, individual leaders were organizing groups of personal followers and beginning to develop varieties of alliances.[b]

Resistance in Eastern Laos

Before 1949 the more important center of activity of the future Pathet Lao organization was in the east. Following the French reestablishment of their rule in Indochina in 1945, the Viet Minh were instrumental in recruiting, training, and organizing Lao participation in an Indochina-wide movement to expel the French. They helped the handful of Lao nationalists to organize guerrilla bands, especially in the areas adjacent to Vietnam, and provided assistance in security, rice, weapons, and money, within the limits of their own meager resources. A few of these Lao bands operated on their own to harass the French colonial authorities and their Lao collaborators; however, most of them served as

[a]Since our previous study includes a history of the Lao revolutionary movement, in this appendix we shall discuss only those factors necessary to understand the emergence of the Pathet Lao leadership. For a more complete account, see Paul F. Langer and Joseph J. Zasloff, NORTH VIETNAM AND THE PATHET LAO–PARTNERS IN THE STRUGGLE FOR LAOS (Cambridge, Mass.: Harvard University Press, 1970), Chapters 3 and 4.

[b]In scrutinizing our diverse sources to develop the following account of the Pathet Lao leadership, we have discovered gaps in our knowledge and discrepancies in precise details such as dates and places of birth. The paucity of written data about the Pathet Lao leaders in particular, and about the Pathet Lao movement in general, makes this inevitable. We have used our best judgment to resolve doubts and discrepancies in biographical information. However, we expect that further research will uncover data to update our account and to correct certain errors of detail.

adjuncts to the more powerful Viet Minh forces, acting for the most part as guides, propagandists, interpreters, and general support troops. Some coherence was given to these Lao guerrilla bands in August 1946, when a "Committee of Lao Resistance in the East" was formed at Vinh in Vietnam. An organizer of that committee (A-24), now an official of the RLG, has given us the following account of its formation, and several former guerrillas (A-14, A-18) who served under its direction have filled in the details.

As part of an effort to build centers of resistance against the French in 1946, Ho Chi Minh invited to a meeting in Hanoi a number of Lao who were in Vietnam at the time and who, through his urging, formed the Committee of Lao Resistance in the East. A former Pathet Lao cadre (A-14) who was present at the meeting listed the following officers of the committee (his spelling has been retained when the identity of the individual listed was not certain):

Nouhak Phongsavan	President
O Anourak	Vice-President; Commander of Forces
Som Phommachanh	Administrative Director
Pho Luanglao	Treasurer
Ma (Khaitkhamphithoune)	Committeeman
Faydang	Committeeman of Lao Soung
Boun Lieng	Committeeman
Apheui (Keobounheuang)	Committeeman of Lao Theung

Each member of the committee was to supervise a number of branches, each with the objective of enlarging the nationalist movement in his region of operation. The branches included the following:

Sam Thay Branch in Sam Neua Province

Ma	Chairman
King Vorasane	Vice Chairman
Ke	Military Committeeman

Muong Sene Branch (Vietnam) in Xieng Khouang Province

Faydang	Chairman
Nhia Vu	Vice Chairman
(Thit) Khamphong	Committeeman
Nha Foung	Committeeman (Secretary)

Tha Fai Ban Branch (set up in Chu Lai, Vietnam) for Khammouane Province (Thakek)

Say Phetrasy	Chairman

Tasseng of Tha Fai Ban	Vice Chairman
Village Chief of	
Ban Sop Khone	Committeeman

Boualapha Branch (Headquarters in Phu Trat, Vietnam) for Savannakhet Province

O (Anourak)	Chairman
Lao	Vice Chairman
Alpheui	
(Keobounheuang)	Committeeman

The committee headquarters was situated in a Viet Minh base area, relied upon the Viet Minh for security, guidance, and communications, and often worked through Viet Minh advisers assigned to many of the regional guerrilla bands in Laos. According to a Viet Minh publication, this committee launched military attacks along Route 7 (a major route leading from North Laos to North Vietnam) in October 1946, and, in January 1947, in Sam Neua Province, from which they were forced to withdraw, "leaving behind a number of cadres to create military bases."[1] This alliance with the Viet Minh, who are not only advisers but also the major source of arms and supplies to the regional bands, gave the committee added control over the local guerrillas in Laos, though it opened the committee to the challenge that it was principally serving the interests of the Vietnamese Communists. While this committee was successful in imposing a measure of cohesion among the scattered guerrilla bands, there still appeared to be loosely connected groups who were loyal primarily to particular regional leaders. We have learned from interviews with members of these bands that in this formative period of the Pathet Lao movement there was considerable infighting among a number of leaders for control and loyalty of the guerrilla groups.[2]

Some guerrilla commanders who had established a strong political base in their native areas became identified with the eastern group. Faydang, a prominent Meo leader, and his younger brother, Nhia Vu, both Meo from Xieng Khouang Province, were drawn into the Committee of Lao Resistance in the East in its initial stage, and were officially designated as officers of their local Muong Sene branch, no doubt to rally support among the important Meo tribal groups. Faydang, then serving as a village head man,[3] began organizing Meo into guerrilla units against the French in 1945 or 1946.[4] Interviews with Meo witnesses suggest that Faydang was probably driven less by his animosity toward the French or his affection for either the Lao or Vietnamese nationalists than by his own struggle for power within the Meo community with his nephew, Touby Ly Foung, both members of the Ly clan. (Touby Lyfong, considered paramount chief of the Meo, was one of the first of his tribe to receive a Westernized higher education. He is currently a prominent Meo leader on the RLG side.) Another charter member of the Muong Sene branch of the Committee of Lao Resistance in the East was Lo Foung Pablia,[c] also a member of a prominent Meo family. Some thirteen years the junior of Faydang, Lo Foung has not had the public prominence of Faydang or his brother, but he and the two others were named to the Central Committee of the Neo Lao Issara, formed in 1950.

Sithon Kommadam was another one of those leaders who strengthened the Lao resistance in the east with the tribesmen he had organized in southern Laos. His father, Kommadam, a chieftain from the Boloven mountain area in southern Laos,[5] had led a revolt against the French in 1935[6] and was executed in 1937. Sithon, born in Attopeu Province in 1910, was imprisoned and tortured by the French after his father's execution, according to the Australian Communist journalist Wilfred Burchett.[7] Although the full details of his recruitment into the Lao nationalist movement are not clear, the evidence suggests that at an early stage the Viet Minh had developed close ties with him. His family history indicates that he would be strongly motivated to contribute his talents to a rebellion against the French. In the early years of the Lao resistance movement, emissaires both from the east and from the Issara government maintained contact with him, but he appears to have been dominated by neither. Because of his anti-French sentiments and his close ties with the Viet Minh, it is not surprising that after 1949 he threw in his lot with the eastern resistance group. Since then Kommadam has been the leading Lao Theung member of the Pathet Lao leadership group.

Nouhak Phongsavan, it appears, emerged with the greatest power within the eastern sphere. From modest beginnings he built a prosperous trucking business of his own in the prewar period, operating in Laos and Vietnam, where he lived part of the time. According to a Lao friend who knew him in Vietnam during those years, Nouhak became an arms supplier for the Viet Minh toward the end of World War II. Partly from conviction and partly from persuasion by Ho Chi Minh, Nouhak was gradually drawn further into the Viet Minh movement. He was urged by Ho, during the meeting in Hanoi in 1946 which we have described above, to participate in the formation of the Lao Committee of Resistance in the East.

Another leader whose frequent activities in Vietnam during this period identify him with the eastern group, although he was not a member of the Lao Resistance Committee of the East, was Kaysone Phomvihan. Kaysone, who was in his twenties during the early years of the resistance and later rose to a key leadership role within the Pathet Lao, had from the beginning strong ties with the Vietnamese. He was born in the same Mekong River town as Nouhak, in

---

[c]Also known as Fung and Kham Thong. The spelling of Meo names often varies, and it has not always been possible to verify the spelling of a particular name. In case of doubt, the spelling used by the source has been retained.

Savannakhet, southern Laos, the only son of a Lao mother and Vietnamese father, Nguyen Tri Loan, who had served in the colonial administration as a secretary to the French Resident in Savannakhet. Kaysone had his early education in Savannakhet, then went to Hanoi where he completed the first and second part of the baccalaureate, a substantial achievement for a young Lao. He continued in his studies at the Faculty of Medicine (and possibly law) at the University of Hanoi, where he took part in nationalist activities with other students at the university. While in Vietnam, he reportedly developed a close relationship with Vo Nguyen Giap, the future Viet Minh commander-in-chief, as well as with Ho Chi Minh, who felt a great attachment to him.[8]

Kaysone met Souphanouvong in Savannakhet in 1945. Having already organized a small group of followers, Kaysone reportedly put his group under the leadership of Souphanouvong and followed him to Thailand.[9] He was later dispatched by Souphanouvong to Hanoi where he appears to have been instrumental in obtaining Vietnamese funds for the Lao resistance movement. An organizer of the Commitee of Resistance of the East told us he met Kaysone together with Ho Chi Minh at the 1946 meeting in Hanoi, described above. He invited Kaysone to join in the Committee of Resistance, but Kaysone, though sympathetic, had duties to perform for Souphanouvong and chose not to join at the time.

Resistance in Thailand

The Lao Issara leaders who remained in exile in Thailand until 1949 came principally from the upper classes. Their senior leader was Prince Phetsarath, scion of the Vang Na (King of the Front) branch of the royal family of Luang Prabang and formally acknowledged as viceroy (maha ouparat), second man of the realm. The prime minister of their newly established government-in-exile, Phaya (Phagna) Khammao Vilay, was an aristocrat, and almost every member of the cabinet was descended from one of the many noble families of Laos. (The royal families of Luang Prabang and Champassak, and principal families in several other provinces, provided an abundance of nobility for such a little country.) Most of those who did not come from the Lao aristocracy were sons of the more prosperous families of Laos, who could afford to send their sons to the French schools in Vientiane, Luang Prabang, Savannakhet, and Pakse, and frequently for higher education in Hanoi or Saigon.

In these French colonial schools of Indochina, the Lao elite were exposed to the same nationalist "germs" as were their Vietnamese classmates. Nevertheless, the nationalism of most of these Lao Issara leaders did not reach the intensity, or the virulence, of that of the Vietnamese. Although there was a widespread feeling that the French should delegate more power to the Lao and also should permit Laos to be united, their resentment and apprehensions were directed equally, if not more, toward the Vietnamese who filled the positions immediately under the French, occupied a majority of the places in the French schools in Laos and, along with Chinese merchants, dominated urban life. Moreover, although these Lao held a certain admiration for the Vietnamese nationalist movement, they were offended by what they regarded as swaggering Viet Minh nationalists in Laos, and were fearful that a Vietnamese success in expelling the French would leave Laos dominated by Vietnam. Indeed, the Lao were ambivalent about their anti-French nationalism. Many saw the French as protectors of the Lao against their two traditional enemies, the Vietnamese and the Thai, who in the past had absorbed significant segments of Laos.[10] The consolidation of power by the Communists in China in 1949 caused apprehension among the petty nobility of little Laos. Surrounded as they were by potential enemies, it is no wonder that many of the Issara elite favored only a gradual French devolution of power, if they were to be the recipients of this power, and wished for some continued French presence, particularly for French material aid.

Not all of the Lao upper classes, of course, had joined the Lao Issara. The king had remained in Luang Prabang and was maintained in a symbolic role by the French colonial regime. Many members of powerful families—Boun Oum na Champassak in the south, for one—participated in the governments established by the French. There was constant contact between the Lao Issara leaders and their large families, friends, and even political competitors who remained in Laos. By 1948, the Issara government-in-exile agreed that one of their best educated and able members, Nhouy Abhay, should return to Vientiane and join the Boun Oum government, which governed under French tutelage. With Nhouy as emissary, a plan for national reconciliation was worked out with the French, and, in 1949, a majority of the Lao Issara leaders accepted the French offer of quasi-autonomy, to be gradually expanded, and returned to Laos. The Issara leaders who returned to Vientiane (among them the present Prime Minister Souvanna Phouma) appeared satisfied with the increased political role offered to them by the French. While their upper-class origins, on one hand, made them feel that they were the natural rulers of Laos, they were nevertheless not confident enough of their ability, or their resources, to rule Laos without outside assistance.

The Lao Issara leaders had expressed their nationalism by organizing themselves, seeking exile in Thailand, and harassing the French until they received concessions. But, as we have shown, most were not virulently anti-French. Moreover, they missed their large families and their homeland. We do not demean the patriotism or the courage of these leaders in observing that they had their fill of life in exile. They could see independence arriving gradually under the French program. Endowed with the Lao qualities of good humor, flexibility, and unaggressiveness, they did not wish to emulate their more impassioned neighbors, the Viet Minh, in committing themselves to a protracted guerrilla struggle. True, the Issara had organized clusters of small bands to harass the French before 1949, but the level of violence they produced was quite low, compared with that of the Viet Minh. The concessions they had achieved were sufficient, they judged, for them to end their lonely exile and join with those leaders who had stayed on without interruption to cooperate with the French in the Vientiane government.

The refusal by some to return to Laos with the Lao Issara leaders constituted a fundamental split in Lao political loyalties: the majority group, "moderates," were willing to accept limited autonomy under French tutelage; a minority group, the "militants," threw in their lot with the Viet Minh and continued to struggle against the French. Despite several agreements for reconciliation, this split has persisted until the present; the moderates provide the major segment of the Royal Lao Government leadership in Vientiane and derive outside support from the United States and Thailand; and the militants provide the Pathet Lao leadership and draw their support from North Vietnam and the Communist powers.

We have told the story, in our earlier study, of Prince Souphanouvong's refusal to join his Issara colleagues in accepting the French offer to return. A number of the Issara members in Thailand followed his lead and joined forces with the resistance group in the east—essentially committing themselves to serve with the Viet Minh. Phoumi Vongvichit, who was to become an important leader in the Pathet Lao movement, broke with the Lao Issara government along with Souphanouvong and has remained one of his closest collaborators. Born about 1910 in Xieng Khouang, the son of a governor of Vientiane Province, Phoumi attended the College Pavie in Vientiane, through which many of the Lao elite had passed. After passing an examination to enter into the colonial administration he served as district chief (chao muong) in both Xieng Khouang and Vientiane Provinces from 1940 to 1945.[d] In 1945, the French authorities appointed him governor (chao khoueng) of Sam Neua Province. About 1945, he entered into liaison with the Viet Minh, and in 1946 he fled to Thailand where he worked with the Lao Issara government until 1949.

Another who followed Souphanouvong's route was Prince (Tiao) Souk Vongsak. Born into the royal family in Luang Prabang about 1915, he attended school in Luang Prabang (as a classmate of Prince Somsanith, a Lao Issara minister in Thailand and later a prime minister in Vientiane). Souk entered the colonial administration and served, before 1945, as a functionary in the royal palace in Luang Prabang and as an administrator in Xieng Khouang Province. In 1945, according to one report, he was appointed district chief of Paksane by the Japanese, who had defeated and replaced the French, but he worked secretly with the guerrillas in the area. The next year he fled to Thailand to join the Lao

[d] In 1941, according to one report, he joined a pro-French, nationalist movement against Thailand, later known as the Movement for Lao National Renovation (Mouvement de Rénovation Nationale Lao).

Issara. For a time he served as private secretary to Phaya Khammao Vilay, prime minister of the Lao Issara government.

Souk appears to have left Thailand from time to time on missions to various guerrilla groups in eastern Laos. One interviewee told us of his meeting with Souk in 1948, when the latter was in Vietnam on a liaison mission for the Lao Issara group. According to this account, Souk's life was in danger from guerrillas under the command of Phoumi Nosavan, who was then attempting to consolidate troops independent of the Issara in Thailand. Souk's mission, it appears, was to prevent this action, and he was lucky to escape with his life.

Still another upper-class member of the Lao Issara group who threw in his lot with the east was Singkapo Chounramany. Born in February 1913 in the Mekong River town of Thakhek, in southern Laos, Singkapo was a member of one of the leading families of Laos which had administered Khammouane Province for three generations. A schoolteacher until 1945, Singkapo joined the Lao Issara in 1945 and commanded their forces at Thakhek. After the capture of Thakhek in 1946 by the French, he fled into Thailand with Souphanouvong.[11]

Singkapo and Phoumi Nosavan were childhood friends, perhaps cousins, and were closely linked during these early days of the nationalist movement. Singkapo traveled to the eastern region with Phoumi, apparently engaged in an effort, described above, to win over troops and guerrilla bands led by others and to consolidate leadership independent of the Lao Issara. Though we lack precise details of this enterprise, it fits into the general picture of the scramble for power by individual leaders among disparate guerrilla bands. Whatever the details were of this political manipulation, it appears that Singkapo remained in the east and Phoumi Nosavan returned to Thailand. Though Singkapo in earlier days had a reputation for playboy inclinations and bourgeois tastes, he has remained an active and royal Pathet Lao leader, serving today as commander of the Lao People's Liberation Army forces in Xieng Khouang area.

Consolidation of the Pathet Lao Leadership

Following the official dissolution of the Lao Issara government in October 1949, Prince Souphanouvong with a number of his followers journeyed to the Viet Minh headquarters at Tuyen Quang, North Vietnam, to meet Ho Chi Minh and to negotiate for Viet Minh support. From this time on, with close Viet Minh guidance, the remaining Lao resistance movement, soon to be called the Pathet Lao, began the development of a set of political and administrative institutions that had more similarity—at least in form—to their DRV model than to their Lao counterpart in Vientiane.

In the summer of 1950, not long after his meeting with Ho, Souphanouvong convoked "the First Resistance Congress" of Laos. This was a meeting of some 105 representatives, particularly from the eastern regions of Laos adjacent to

Vietnam. A majority of the members of the congress had been associated with the Committee of Resistance in the East, though Souphanouvong's colleagues from Thailand were also present.[12] This congress, guided by Viet Minh advisers, announced on August 16, 1950, the formation of the Neo Lao Issara (meaning, "Free Laos Front"), and dropped the label "Lao Issara" which they had continued to use after the return of the exile government in Thailand to Laos. This new political organization was modeled on the Viet Minh Patriotic Front and was directed by a Central Committee.

The congress also announced a new "Resistance Government," composed of the following members:[13]

Souphanouvong	Premier (and Foreign Minister)
Phoumi Vongvichit	Deputy Prime Minister and Minister for Internal Affairs
Kaysone	Minister of Defense
Nouhak	Minister of Finance
Souk Vongsak	Minister of Education
Sithon Kommadam	Minister Without Portfolio (Tribal Affairs)
Faydang	Minister Without Portfolio (Tribal Affairs)

The resistance government and the front announced in Vietnam contained the key leaders of the Pathet Lao who have remained the most important personalities of the Lao Communist movement. (Although all of the members of the resistance government have remained prominent, some of the early members of the front have passed into obscurity.) Possibly our frequent reference to the ministerial titles that these leaders distributed among themselves might conjure up the image of importance conveyed by these titles in larger, established governments. It should be kept in mind that these leaders constituted a small number of revolutionaries—considered by the Lao Issara majority as a rump group—with control in the early years over a relative handful of inhabitants in the remote and more primitive highland areas of Laos.

Profiles of Three PL Leaders

Kaysone Phomvihan

The person many observers have designated as the most powerful leader in the Lao Communist movement during the past few years is Kaysone Phomvihan. There were reports in early January 1969 that Kaysone had been killed in a bombing raid somewhere in Sam Neua Province in August 1968. Refugees apparently spoke of Kaysone's death to Royal Lao Government military officials, who first broadcasted it over the RLG radio.[14] For a full year after his reported death, Kaysone's name was not mentioned, whereas formerly he had been cited as being present at public ceremonies and giving speeches or sending messages to foreign governments. It must therefore be assumed that either illness or an accident removed him temporarily from the scene, since in the fall of 1969 Kaysone's name was once more in the news.[15]

As the son of a Vietnamese father who served as a secretary to the French Resident in Savannakhet, Kaysone did not have the social attributes for status among the lowland Lao. His ascendancy within the Pathet Lao power structure must be attributed to his close links with the Vietnamese Communists, though this relationship should not obscure his reputation for intelligence and competence. Since he was half Vietnamese, spoke Vietnamese as his mother tongue, and had his secondary school and university education in Hanoi, it is not surprising that he developed strong Vietnamese ties.

An RLG official who knew Kaysone as a student in Hanoi said that one of Kaysone's teachers at his lycée in Hanoi was Vo Nguyen Giap, and other reports support the claim that Kaysone developed a friendship with Giap. As mentioned above, Kaysone is also said to have grown close, in personal terms, to Ho Chi Minh. These early relationships endured and help account for his rapid movement up the ladder of Pathet Lao power in the two decades following 1950. Kaysone is said to have joined the Indochinese Communist Party (ICP) in 1946, one of the first Lao to do so, and became a member of the Lao Dong party when it replaced the ICP in 1951.[16] Kaysone was publicly acknowledged as the secretary-general of the Central Committee of the People's Party of Laos in July 1967,[17] a strong basis for assuming he is among the most powerful leaders, if not the single most important one, in the PL movement.

At the formation of the initial "Resistance Government" in August 1950, Kaysone, then only twenty-five (or possibly thirty) years old, was named minister of defense, and was also a member of the Neo Lao Issara Central Committee. In a small, fledgling organization a "minister of defense" performs many functions. Kaysone served as commander-in-chief of the PL troops for a time and set up and directed, in 1950 to 1951, what came to be known as the Kommadam Military Training School, the training institution for most future PL officers. Since the PL military were dependent upon the Viet Minh from 1950 to 1954, and were integrated into the Viet Minh operation, Kaysone continued his close relations with the Viet Minh leaders. Indeed, his headquarters was located during most of that period within North Vietnam.[18]

During the years from 1954 to 1957, Kaysone retained his primary military role within the Pathet Lao. In addition, he participated in negotiating the Geneva Agreements, was a member of the PL delegation to the initial conferences at Khang Khay in January 1955, and in April and May took part in negotiations in Vientiane on the issue of integration with the RLG. Also in

1955, he made one of his rare trips out of Southeast Asia to attend the World Peace Congress in Helsinki. In August 1956, he was the principal negotiator with the RLG. When negotiations reached an agreement on integration of the PL with the Vientiane government, supplementary elections for seats in the National Assembly were held in May 1958. Kaysone ran as a candidate in Attopeu Province and was defeated.[19]

Ironically, Kaysone's failure to win a seat in the RLG National Assembly in 1958 seems ultimately to have advanced his political career within the Pathet Lao. He was not present in Vientiane when sixteen of the key Lao Patriotic Front leaders, including seven who had been elected to the National Assembly,[e] were imprisoned on charges of treason by the right-wing Phoui Sananikone government when it came to power in 1959. In the months from July 1959 to May 1960, when his colleagues were in prison, Kaysone was the senior member of the Pathet Lao. This provided him the opportunity to be the principal PL decision maker at a crucial time in Lao political history. There was turbulence in Vientiane and the North Vietnamese were taking an increasingly active role in Lao internal affairs with the launching of stronger North Vietnamese-Pathet Lao military initiatives. In a country where age commands respect, Kaysone's youth, relative to his colleagues, may have marginally checked his rise to the peak of power until then, but by July 1959 when circumstances brought him heavy responsibility he was at least thirty-four and had fourteen years of experience in the PL movement. Since then, Kaysone has unquestionably been one of the most important PL leaders and probably its most influential individual.

Following the escape of the NLHS (Neo Lao Hak Sat, or Lao Patriot Front) leaders from prison in July 1960, a new PL government was established in a PL-controlled zone (the previous PL government was dissolved in 1957 when the integration arrangement was concluded) and Kaysone resumed his official title of minister of defense. Though some of the PL leaders returned to Vientiane after the Kong Le coup in August 1960, Kaysone was not reported to have been among them; apparently he was directing affairs in the PL zone and traveling to Vietnam. It is characteristic of his career during the 1960s that he remained close to or in Vietnam, leaving official contacts with the RLG to Souphanou-vong and other colleagues.

Nouhak Phongsavan

Another leader at the top of the Pathet Lao power structure with Kaysone is Nouhak Phongsavan. Like Kaysone he was born in Savannakhet, but he was the son of lowland Lao peasant parents. With no more traditional political base than Kaysone, his rise in influence must also be attributed in good part to the close relations he developed with Viet Minh leaders beginning in the 1940s. Nouhak's

---

[e]Souphanouvong, Phoumi Vongvichit, Nouhak Phoagsavan, Sithon Kommadam, Phoun Sipraseut, Khamphay Boupha, Sisana Sisane.

first Viet Minh contact came not, as did Kaysone's, through education—Nouhak completed only primary school in Savannakhet—but through business contacts as a mature merchant. (He is some ten years older than Kaysone.)

Nouhak's first job when he left Savannakhet as a young man was in Khammouane Province in the Boneng mines, where he supervised coolies. He became a truck driver and, in 1938, returned to Savannakhet where he was hired by a Chinese merchant to transport freight and passengers over the colonial route between Savannakhet and Dong Ha in Central Vietnam. During the hostilities between France and Thailand in 1939 and 1940, while he was still working as a trucker, Nouhak trafficked in contraband merchandise. At some point he developed a transport business of his own and by 1941 he had good contacts in Vietnam with merchants in Tourane, Hue, and Hanoi. From 1943 to 1945, he expanded his commerce to include the sale of Chinese nationalist currency, buying it at the North Vietnam port of Haiphong and then driving through Savannakhet to Thailand, where he exchanged it in Bangkok for gold ingots. He picked up cardamom and kerosene in Thailand and transported these back for sale in Vietnam. While on a business trip in Tourane at the time of the Japanese coup on March 9, 1945, he was blocked from Laos and remained in Vietnam until the Japanese surrender.

As mentioned earlier, Nouhak was also engaged in commerce in arms toward the end of World War II. He came to know Ho Chi Minh, Pham Van Dong, Tran Huy Lieu,[20] and other Viet Minh leaders, who persuaded him to become an arms supplier for them and gradually drew him into the Viet Minh movement.

These business links with the Viet Minh were reinforced by other aspects of Nouhak's personal life. Before 1945, Nouhak had a Lao wife, Bounthom, with whom he had at least one daughter.[21] He last saw his first wife in 1945. While in Vietnam he took a second wife, a Vietnamese, Chu Thich, with whom he had at least one son. (Nouhak speaks Vietnamese fluently.) Finally, one report states that Nouhak's brother was killed by the French in a battle as they were reimposing their colonial rule following their defeat by the Japanese. The loss of his brother was said to have embittered Nouhak and impelled him further toward the Viet Minh cause. Nouhak is said to have joined the Indochinese Communist party in 1949 and to be a member of its successor, the Lao Dong party.

We have described his leadership role in establishing the Committee of Lao Resistance of the East in 1946 at the urging of Ho Chi Minh. When the first resistance government was proclaimed in 1950, Nouhak, because of his past experience, was designated the minister of finance. He was also a member of the Central Committee that founded the Neo Lao Issara and has served on the Central Committee of the NLHS, its successor, until the present. In 1952, Nouhak attended, along with Souphanouvong, Kaysone, and Sisana Sisane, the Tuyen Quang meeting in North Vietnam which established the Lao-Viet-Khmer front.

Near the top of the PL power structure from the outset, Nouhak has had an important role in negotiations, both within Laos and in foreign affairs. He was officially designated minister of foreign affairs some time before April 1954, taking over this post from Souphanouvong who had handled the foreign affairs portfolio as well as being prime minister. In his diplomatic capacity Nouhak attended the Peiping Peace Conference in October 1952 and the Vienna Peace Congress in November 1952, returning in 1953 to Vietnam. At various times during this journey he visited Prague, Bucharest, Moscow, and North Korea. In May 1954, he appeared at the Geneva Conference as a member of the DRV delegation.

Negotiating on questions internal to Laos, together with Phoumi Vongvichit and Singkapo he represented the PL at the talks with the RLG at Khang Khay from December 1954 to January 1955. In May 1955 he was a member of the PL permanent political delegation in Vientiane and in October 1955 he was on the PL delegation to the Rangoon talks with the RLG, along with Prince Souphanouvong, Phoumi Vongvichit, and Singkapo.

By mid-1956, Nouhak headed the PL permanent delegation in Vientiane and under Phoumi Vongvichit was deputy leader of the political element of the joint political and military delegation in talks with the RLG which started in September 1956.

When negotiations for integration with the Royal Lao Government came to fruition in 1957, and supplementary elections for the National Assembly were held in 1958, Nouhak, like Kaysone, posed his candidature for a seat not in his birthplace of Savannakhet, where his family was not prominent, but in Sam Neua, a Pathet Lao stronghold. Sam Neua Province, adjacent to North Vietnam, had served as a regroupment zone for Viet Minh and Pathet Lao soldiers following the Geneva Agreements of 1954, and the Pathet Lao maintained headquarters and exercised strong political influence in the area even after integration with the RLG. Nouhak was elected, and took his seat in Vientiane. Like the other PL members of the National Assembly in Vientiane he was followed, and often harassed, by right-wing agents and police. Nouhak was among the sixteen Pathet Lao leaders who were arrested in July 1959; he escaped in May 1960 to security in the Pathet Lao base area in the east.

In the new NLHS government of 1960, Nouhak occupied the post of minister of agriculture. Following Kong Le's coup d'état in August 1960, which changed the political climate in Vientiane, Nouhak briefly returned to Vientiane as a member of a PL delegation to conduct negotiations with the RLG. On October 31, 1960, Nouhak had been announced publicly as vice-chairman of the Committee for Peace, Neutrality, National Concord, and Unification. The climate in Vientiane changed once again in December 1960, when Phoumi Nosavan and Boun Oum seized power and Nouhak fled with the Communists and neutralists. In March 1961 Nouhak attended a session of the World Council of Peace, held at New Delhi. The countercoup by Phoumi Nosavan's right-wing forces led again to hostilities and brought a renewed flurry of negotiations, both internal and international. Nouhak headed the NLHS delegation to the Ban Namone talks and served on Souphanouvong's delegation to the Vientiane princes' meeting in January 1962.

At the various negotiations concerning the creation of a coalition government following the Geneva Agreements of 1962, the PL delegation pressed for the inclusion of Nouhak as a minister in Vientiane, without success. It is not clear why RLG negotiators objected to him. He may have been considered by some as a hard-core Communist, firmly under the domination of the North Vietnamese. Some may have felt offended by the inclusion of what they regarded as a lower-class Lao to participate in their upper-class government. We noted in our discussions with RLG leaders that Nouhak was frequently referred to with a certain air of derision as a former "commerçant" or, as one Lao nobleman who had negotiated on the other side of the table from him at Rangoon put it, "un simple transporteur."

Nouhak remains one of the most important men in the Lao Communist movement, one whose power will be enhanced if Kaysone should go into an eclipse as he did during 1968/69. Nouhak is regarded by many observers as the political commander of the PL movement. He is a permanent member of the Central Committee of the Lao Patriotic Front and is reported to be a first secretary of the Central Committee of the People's Party of Laos as well as a continuing member of the Lao Dong party.

Prince Souphanouvong[22]

From the NLHS beginnings, Prince Souphanouvong has been presented publicly, both to the Lao people and internationally, as the most important figure in the movement. He was chairman of the First Resistance Congress, which met in 1950, chairman of the Central Committee of the Neo Lao Issara formed in the same year, and prime minister of the first Pathet Lao government in 1950. At a meeting late in 1950 of representatives of the three Indochinese liberation movements (where Ton Duc Thang, in 1969 successor to Ho Chi Minh as president of the DRV, was the Vietnamese representative), Prince Souphanouvong represented Laos. He continued to serve as head of the successors to that Pathet Lao government, and has been chairman of the Central Committee of each successive front organization. In messages to foreign chiefs of state over the past two decades, Prince Souphanouvong has been the chief spokesman of the Pathet Lao, both sending and receiving messages in the name of the Pathet Lao. This titular leadership is acknowledged by the Vietnamese, Chinese, and Soviets, who frequently use the formula in their communications, "under the leadership of Prince Souphanouvong." He has generally been the chief negotiator with the RLG when the central issue of political reconciliation has been raised: in Geneva in 1954; at the integration negotiations in 1957; and in Geneva in 1962 as well as at its preceding conferences. In the agreement to form a coalition government in 1962, when Prince Souvana Phouma as the neutralist was named as prime minister, Souphanouvong was named as deputy prime minister along with Phoumi Nosavan, representative of the right-wing forces. Purely on the basis of the important functions he has performed, it is clear that Souphanouvong has occupied a central position in the constellation of Pathet Lao power. In addition, on the basis of his national prominence as a member of the royal family, his impressive personal qualities of energy and intelligence, and his longevity in the revolutionary movement, Prince Souphanouvong must be ranked among the most important and popular[f] personalities in the Pathet Lao movement.

Nevertheless, it is the opinion of many, both within the Pathet Lao movement (according to the testimony of former Pathet Lao) and among neutralists who for a time cooperated closely with them, that Souphanouvong does not perform the key decision-making function. Indeed, in the view of some, he has been for years a figurehead, manipulated by the Vietnamese and their chosen Lao leaders, because of his name and traditional status in Lao society. According to this view, the more important leaders are Kaysone and Nouhak, both of whom are more trusted by the Vietnamese. These leaders, and others, operate from within the semisecret People's Party of Laos (PPL), with the support, of course, of their North Vietnamese mentors.

Although categorically we can neither confirm nor deny this hypothesis, we can provide some perspective to the varied assessments of Souphanouvong's leadership role. Souphanouvong actually does not have the authority and influence suggested by the public pronouncements from PL headquarters in Sam Neua or the propaganda from Hanoi, Peking, and other capitals in the Communist world. In Communist regimes the political party has always been the key source of power. Souphanouvong is now mentioned as being a member of the PPL, yet most reports suggest that he does not have longevity in the party equivalent to that of other important leaders and does not occupy a key post in its hierarchy. It is true that the PPL is relatively new and that is has not yet assumed the open leadership role that its model, the Lao Dong party, plays in North Vietnam. Nevertheless, it seems likely that as the PPL has grown into the ruling instrument, particularly in the past five years, Souphanouvong's own leadership role has proportionately diminished. Moreover, as long as Prince Souphanouvong was operating as a leader of the Pathet Lao political forces within the RLG context—from 1957 to 1959 during the attempted integration and from 1962 to 1964 during the post-Geneva tripartite government—his decision-making power was clearly enhanced. He was certainly influenced by other leaders in the movement and by Viet Minh advisers, but his role in the

---

[f]In the 1952 election, for example, Prince Souphanouvong polled more votes than any other candidate.

tripartite government, and his physical presence in Vientiane, gave him a measure of independence from other PL leaders and the Vietnamese. He does not enjoy that independence now, operating out of the Pathet Lao zone where Vietnamese advisers are strategically placed throughout the Pathet Lao decision-making framework and, significantly, where there are an estimated 40,000 to 60,000 North Vietnamese troops.

Although Souphanouvong's power is limited, the available evidence does not lead us to conclude that his role is that of a mere figurehead. Rather, we conclude that Souphanouvong remains an influential, though probably not the primary, decision maker among the Pathet Lao elite.

Appendix B: Members of the Central Committee of the Neo Lao Hak Sat in 1950, 1956, and 1964

1950	1956	1964
Souphanouvong	Souphanouvong	Souphanouvong
Sithon Kommadam	Sithon Kommadam	Sithon Kommadam
Faydang	Faydang	Faydang
Kaysone	Kaysone	Kaysone
Phoumi Vongvichit	Phoumi Vongvichit	Phoumi Vongvichit
	Am Lo	Am Lo
	Am Vu	Am Vu
	Apheuy Keobounheuang	Apheuy Keobounheuang
Ba Noi	Ba Noi	
	Boun (Khongboun)	Boun (Khongboun)
	Bounthay (Nang)	Bounthay (Nang)
	Chalen Sotsisana (by 1959)	Chaleun Sotsisana
Khamfeuan Tounalom	Khamfeuan Tounalom	
	Khamla (Nang)	Khamla (Nang)
	Ka Lang (by 1959)	Ka Lang
	Khamphai Boupha	Khamphai Boupha
	Khampang Boupha (Nang)	Khampang Boupha (Nang)
	Khamphet Phoummavan (by 1959)	Khamphet Phoummavan
	Khamphan Vanavong (Phra Maha)	Phamphan Vanavong (Phra Maha)
	Kham Phoumi	Kham Phoumi
	Khamtay Siphandone	Khamtay Siphandone
	Kongsy (Phra Maha)	Kongsy (Phra Maha)
Lofoung Pablia	Lofoung Pablia	Lofoung Pablia
Ma	Ma	Ma
May Khamdi	May Khamdi (killed 1959)	
	May Souk	May Souk
Mun	Mun	Mun
Nhia Vu Bliayao	Nhia Vu Bliayao	Nhia Vu Bliayao
Nouhak Phongsavan	Nouhak Phongsavan	Nouhak Phongsavan
	Phao Phimmachan (by 1959)	Phao Phimmachan
	Pho Pheng	Pho Pheng
	Phoun Sipraseut	Phoun Sipraseut
	Phomma Douangmala	Phomma Douangmala
Singkapo Chounramany	Singkapo Chounramany	Singkapo Chounramany
Sisana Sisane		Sisana Sisane
	Sisavat	Sisavat
	Sisomphone	Sisomphone
Som Phommachan	Som Phommachan	Som Phommachan
	Sisomphone	Sisomphone

---

aIt is possible that there are inaccuracies in these lists.

1950	1956	1964
Souk Vongsak	Souk Vongsak	Souk Vongsak
	Thavone	Thavone
Thit Mouan	Thit Mouan Saochanthala	Thit Mouan Saochanthala
	Thong Chanh Ouplavan	Thong Chanh Ouplavan
	(by 1959)	

1. To unite all the people, unite various nationalities, strata, religious communities, political parties, patriotic personalities, and intellectuals, including individuals in the Royal Family and Buddhist monks and nuns who favor peace and neutrality, regardless of their political tendencies, beliefs, and religion, also organizations and individuals who were formerly forced by the United States to follow it but now favor a policy of peace and neutrality; and to strive to consolidate and strengthen the alliance and mutual assistance between the NLHS and the patriotic Neutralist forces.

2. To struggle against the U.S. imperialists and their followers—the traitors—for a correct implementation of the 1962 Geneva Agreements and the Zurich and Plaine des Jarres joint communiqués, and the agreements reached between the three Laotian parties; to defend and consolidate the Coalition Government so as to fully carry out the political program aimed at restoring peace, building national concord, and consolidating the independence of the country; first of all to demand that the U.S. imperialists and their satellites withdraw all their troops from Laos, stop the introduction of weapons and war material into Laos and all acts of intervention in Laotian internal affairs under whatever form and in whatever fields, and not set up military bases on Laotian
··· to demand that the Phoumi Nosavan group put an end to aiding
·pon and terrorizing the people and withdraw their
xisting when the 1962 Geneva Agreements were signed;
umi Nosavan group strictly implement the agreements
three parties, first of all organize the mixed police and
Luang Prabang as to restore the normal activities of the
continue the tripartite negotiations in order to settle
other problems of the fatherland and people.
arry out the policy of peace and neutrality insured by the
implement the independent foreign policy on the basis of
Peaceful Coexistence, to establish diplomatic relations
es on equal footing, receive aid without any conditions
ountries regardless of their political regime, provided the
latter respe   vereignty and independence of Laos and sincerely help Laos'
national construction; to actively support all movements for peace, democracy, and social progress, and the national liberation movement of all the Asian, African, and Latin-American countries, and actively contribute to the safeguarding of peace in southeast Asia and the world.

4. To heighten the spirit of self-reliance and at the same time make full use of assistance without any conditions attached from various countries to build an independent and self-supporting economy under the leadership and unified management of the Coalition Government; to wipe out the vestige of the "Cuong Lam" (local despots) regime and the monopoly in trade, and at the same time to help the people develop production, tap forest products and natural resources, expand the intercourse in goods, develop handicraft, and build an industry; to eliminate speculation and hoarding, oppose corruption and misuse of power to grab goods and economic monopoly, and strive to help the farmers to develop cultivation, livestock breeding, help and encourage the improvement of cultivation and protection of crops, thus helping the farmers to raise their income; to help the workers to get jobs, improve their living conditions, and create a regime of social insurance so as to enable them to restore and develop the national economy; to stimulate and help the traders and industrialists to invest in construction and commerce which benefit the national economy and the people's life; to create conditions for students and pupils to study and develop their ability to serve the fatherland. Intellectuals, office employees, cultural workers, and artists will be provided with suitable jobs and their life will be guaranteed so that they can develop their ability to serve the people.

5. To organize and build a national army and a unified police to defend the independence of the fatherland and the security of the people; to help armymen and policemen come close to and help the people and forbid all repression of the people by the army and police; to insure political rights and due pay to army men; to cancel the regime of ill-treatment of armymen and policemen; to work out a policy to help and improve the living conditions of wounded armymen and war martyrs' families.

6. To carry out all the democratic rights of the citizens as provided for by the 1957 constitution, thus enabling them to devote all their ability to serve national construction; first of all, to release all political detainees and insure the life and property of the people; to stop all acts of discrimination and reprisal against patriotic individuals and organizations in the Savannakhet temporarily controlled areas, especially in Vientiane.

7. To respect and defend the Throne, build and consolidate national solidarity, and realize national harmony and unification; to carry out the policy of national union, thus helping the various nationalities to live on an equal footing and carry out mutual assistance, improving their living conditions, helping each other in study; to oppose all schemes of sowing discord among the nationalities and insure the legitimate rights of foreign residents in Laos.

8. To assure equality between men and women, help women in all fields so as to enable them to develop their ability to catch up with men; help confined mothers and protect children.

9. To develop progressive national culture; pay attention to education, develop primary and secondary education systems and other popular education

schools; help all the people, especially mountain people, to learn to read and write; to protect and develop good ethics; to strictly oppose the depraved and obscurantist culture of the United States and its henchmen; to eliminate gambling and other social vices. To respect freedom of belief, oppose all schemes to sabotage and split up religions; to protect pagodas and respect Buddhist priests.

10. While the U.S. imperialists have not yet given up their schemes to eliminate the Neo Lao Hak Sat and other patriotic forces, turn Laos into a neocolony, a war-provocative base, and turn the Laotian people into their slaves, all Laotian people have the task to strive and defend and consolidate the liberated areas, strengthen the Neo Lao Hak Sat forces, help consolidate other patriotic forces, resolutely smash all schemes to encroach upon and occupy the liberated areas and send bandits to disturb and sabotage these areas. The Laotian people must actively carry out all tasks which benefit the people and must bring them a happy life so as to help them build the liberated areas into a firm basis for the people's struggle for peace, neutrality, independence, democracy, unity, and prosperity.

Appendix D: Twelve-Point Program Adopted by the Third National Congress of the Neo Lao Hak Sat in November 1968

On the basis of the correct line of national salvation already mapped out and in the light of the new developments of the situation, the Laotian Patriotic Front laid down the following policies with a view to attaining at all costs its stated political objective:

Point One

A. To strengthen the militant unity and endeavor to broaden the national united front, and actively mobilize all the forces of the country in order to defeat the U.S. imperialist aggression and overthrow the traitors.

B. To respect and protect the throne, and unite broadly with all organizations, social strata, nationalities, religions and political parties, and all forces and all individuals who love the country and peace and are opposed to the U.S. and their lackeys, so as to build a peaceful, independent, neutral, democratic, united and prosperous Laos.

C. To strengthen and consolidate the militant alliance between the Laotian Patriotic Front and the Patriotic Neutralist Forces.

D. To welcome and support all forces, individuals, personalities, intellectuals, students, soldiers, policemen, and employees of the Vientiane administration who are against U.S. aggression and for freedom, democracy, and justice.

E. To be ready to enter into friendly co-operation and on equal footing with those forces and individuals who have broken with organizations controlled by the U.S. puppets and wish to enter into alliance or co-ordinate action with the Laotian Patriotic Front, or the Patriotic Neutralist Forces with a view to opposing the U.S. imperialists and their henchmen.

Point Two

A. To observe equality in all fields and build the unity and relations of mutual assistance among the various nationalities so as to fight the U.S. together, save the country, and build a happy life for all.

B. To do away with all prejudices, grudges, and contradictions created by the imperialists and their henchmen among the various nationalities in Laos and overcome the differences among the latter. All nationalities are equal in interests and duties in all fields and are duty-bound to build unity, conduct the struggle against the U.S. and its servants and help each other make progress and build the country.

C. To actively assist all nationalities, especially the minorities in developing economy, in study, in improving their material and cultural life, in preserving their own customs and traditional culture, and in combating dangerous diseases detrimental to the national progeny so as to help increase the country's population.

D. To actively form a contingent of cadres and intellectuals of minority origin, thus enabling the national minorities to build a more and more advanced life and join in the management of the country.

Point Three

A. To respect and protect Buddhism, and unite with all religions, thus contributing to realizing national unity and strengthening the national forces against U.S. aggression.

B. To oppose all acts of sabotage by the U.S. imperialists and their henchmen against Buddhism, such as distorting Buddhist catechism, controlling Buddhist monks and forcing them to serve criminal schemes, destroying pagodas or using them to preach decadent American culture, sowing discord among various Buddhist factions, etc.

C. To respect and defend Buddhism, preserve the purity of monks and their right to practice Buddhism, protect pagodas, encourage unity and mutual assistance among monks and believers of various Buddhist factions, and encourage solidarity among the priests and followers of other religions.

Point Four

A. To ensure all democratic liberties of the people and to create conditions for the people to bring into fuller play their role as master of the country and of their destiny.

B. To ensure the rights of Laotian citizens of both sexes to vote and stand for elections, and the freedoms of association, meeting, demonstration, speech, press and belief, and ensure the inviolability of the person, the right of ownership, the right to mail privacy, and the rights to free movement and residence.

C. To oppose unwarranted arrests, terrorist acts, and looting by the henchmen of the U.S. imperialists—especially the policies of discrimination, retaliation and persecution of patriots, the concentration of the people in refugee centers, solidarity villages, rehabilitation zones, etc.—forcible conscription to serve the aggressive [designs?] of the U.S. imperialists and the interests of the henchmen of the U.S., exploitation of manpower, and looting of the people's property, to demand the dismantlement of refugee centers, solidarity villages, rehabilitation zones, etc., and the release of all patriots under detention.

Point Five

A. To achieve equality between men and women, and bring into play the role and all-round capacity of women in the struggle against U.S. aggression, for national salvation, and national construction.

B. To realize equality between men and women in all fields, political, economic, cultural and social, encourage women to take part effectively in activities for national salvation and construction and protect the health of women, expectant mothers, and children.

C. To do away with all acts of contempt or oppression toward women, actively create conditions for women and help them to raise their culture and political level and work in their specialties so they may make worthy contributions to the struggle against U.S. aggression, for national salvation, and in national construction.

D. To train and foster women cadres, including women of minority nationalities, so as to mobilize all the capabilities of women for the revolutionary cause of the whole country.

Point Six

A. To build a people's democratic, national union administration which will ensure national sovereignty and serve the interests of the people.

B. To oppose the scheme of the U.S. imperialists and their lackeys to control the Vientiane administration and use it as an instrument of the U.S. neo-colonialist aggressive policy.

C. To set up a democratic, national union government truly representing the interests of all nationalities and an independent and sovereign Laos, and carry out policies of national construction along the line of peace, independence, neutrality, democracy, unity and prosperity.

D. To hold democratic elections at hamlet and village levels, and to select and appoint truly patriotic and popular representatives to the administration at other levels, in order to best serve the interests of the fatherland and the people.

E. To hold general elections to elect a National Assembly truly representing the interests of the people of all strata and nationalities, in line with the amended election law of 1957.

F. To help the administrative personnel at all levels and of all services to enhance their love for their country and people, heighten their sense of duty and improve their professional standards, combat corruption and the abuse of power to oppress subordinates and exploit the people.

Point Seven

A. To build patriotic and people's armed forces and security forces to defend the country and maintain law and public order.

B. To oppose the scheme of the U.S. imperialists and their henchmen to control the Vientiane army and police and their scheme to turn these forces into a mercenary army for aggression in Laos, to oppose the building of bandit and commando groups by the U.S. imperialists and their henchmen with the aim of looting the people and disturbing public order and security.

C. To build patriotic armed forces comprising the regular army, the regional army, the militia, and the people's police, absolutely loyal to the fatherland, with high fighting capacity, and able to fulfill the duty of saving and defending the country.

D. To help the officers and men of the armed forces and police deepen their love for the country and people, and heighten the sense of discipline and responsibility, pay attention to raising the tactical, technical and cultural standards of the officers and men and improve their material and cultural life, to care for the wounded and the sick armymen, and assist the families of those who fall on the field of honor.

Point Eight

A. To build and develop a national, self-supporting economy, improve step by step the people's living conditions and bring prosperity to the country.

B. To eliminate all forms of economic penetration and retardation by U.S. imperialism, all forms of monopoly and exploitation by the ruling circles who are lackeys of the U.S. imperialists, to ban the use of power to grab land, forests, mountains, rivers, streams, and the vestiges of the forced labor system and to campaign for the reduction of land rents, cattle rents and usury rate.

C. To build an independent, self-supporting and prosperous economy composed of industry, agriculture, forestry, trade, communications and transport, finance . . . on the basis of the full utilization of the great economic potentials of the country and developing the people's spirit of self-reliance along with seeking aid from all countries without political conditions attached, with a view to meeting the urgent requirements of the people's life and national construction.

D. To develop agriculture and forestry. The state will undertake the building of water conservancy projects while guiding and helping the people to expand irrigation, improve the methods of cultivation, animal husbandry, forest exploitation and protection. The state also helps the mountain people of various nationalities to settle in areas with favorable conditions for the stabilization and boosting of production.

E. To actively develop industry and rehabilitate and develop handicrafts. Attention will be paid to all the three aspects: expanding state enterprises, encouraging private investments and encouraging industrialists and traders to build enterprises jointly with the state.

F. To expand home trade and develop foreign trade. The state organizes goods interflow, encourages and helps businessmen expand trade to the remotest areas, applies a correct customs policy in trading with foreign countries.

G. To build a state economy and finance and an independent currency. To work out a fair and reasonable tax policy and a correct monetary and price policy so as to stimulate and develop production, ensure the state budget, and contribute to stabilizing the peoples' life.

H. To expand transport and communications through the country, with special attention to building more roads and transport means in the mountain areas. Along with investing in transport, the state encourages private investments so as to expand the transport service with a view to facilitating the movement of the people and boosting economy and culture.

Point Nine

A. To develop the national progressive culture and education, raise the cultural and scientific standards, expand medical work, and protect the people's health. To oppose the depraved and borrowed culture and the corrupt education aimed at realizing the U.S. imperialists' neo-colonialist policy.

B. To speed up the literacy campaign so as to gradually wipe out illiteracy among the people, restore and vigorously multiply primary and secondary schools, open more vocational schools, build higher learning institutions with a national and progressive content. To use the national language as teaching medium at all levels and branches of education. To send students to study abroad along a correct line so as to better serve the fatherland after their return.

C. To develop a national and progressive culture and art, safeguard the Laotians' fine customs and habits, protect the historical relics of various nationalities, launch a movement for a new, civilized way of life, help a number of nationalities to perfect their written languages and to popularize the standard Laotian spoken and written language. To give particular care and assistance to the intellectuals and cultural and art workers to help them develop their talents in service of the fatherland and people.

D. To actively train and foster medical workers along with building a network of hospitals, dispensaries, maternity houses and innoculation stations from the central down to the lowest levels including those in remote places. To launch a disease prevention movement and a sports and physical culture movement along with striving to eradicate a number of dangerous diseases such as malaria, venereal diseases, and leprosy. To reduce the infantile mortality rate with a view to protecting the people's health and increasing the nation's population.

Point Ten

A. To ensure the people's interests and take care of their life, give relief to victims of accidents and ensure social justice and progress.

B. Peasants of all nationalities will have land to till, the poor and the needy will receive farm tools, and all peasants will be helped and guided in boosting production and in study.

C. Workers and other laboring people in the towns will have their life and jobs secured. Workers, in particular, will be protected by labor laws and social insurance, and, first and foremost, enjoy an equitable and rational wage system and the eight-hour workday with one holiday every week.

D. Employees of both public and private services will be given suitable jobs, conditions to improve their cultural and professional levels continually, and will enjoy an equitable and rational wage system.

E. Demobilized servicemen will be ensured jobs.

F. To do away with famine which is still chronic in some areas, develop mutual assistance among the people of all nationalities and, at the same time, work out a policy to relieve victims of natural calamities, famine, etc., especially war victims.

G. To give the best possible medical care to victims of social diseases and take correct measures to check social evils, reform and give jobs to those spoiled by depraved culture in order to turn them into honest people for the benefit of national construction.

Point Eleven

A. To protect the interests of overseas Laotians and the legitimate interests of foreign residents in Laos, enhance the national pride and uphold the national sovereignty of Laos, and defend overseas Laotians from discrimination, bullying, and arbitrary dispossession of their property.

B. Foreign residents who respect Laos' sovereignty will be properly treated and their legitimate interests will be protected. They will be helped in difficulties, and commended for their contributions to the building of friendship with the Laotian people, and to the defense and construction of Laos.

Point Twelve

A. To carry out a foreign policy of peace, independence, neutrality, solidarity and friendship with the peoples and governments of all peace- and justice-loving countries.

B. To oppose all schemes of intervention and aggression under whatever forms by the imperialists and other aggressive forces against Laos, and apply an independent foreign policy aimed at ensuring the sovereignty, independence, unity and territorial integrity of Laos.

C. To live in peace and friendship, and establish diplomatic relations with those countries which respect the independence, sovereignty and territorial integrity of Laos.

D. To strengthen the friendship and solidarity and lasting cooperation on the principle of equality with the peoples of Vietnam and Cambodia in the resistance to U.S. aggression, for national salvation, in the defense of independence and national sovereignty and for national construction.

E. To respect and scrupulously implement the 1954 and 1962 Geneva Agreements on Laos, respect and scrupulously implement all agreements signed with other countries in conformity with the interests of Laos, and abolish all treaties that run counter to the national interests of Laos.

F. Not to join any military alliances, not to allow any foreign country to establish military bases in Laos or use Laotian territory for the purpose of aggression against other countries, not to accept protection by any aggressive military bloc.

G. To strengthen friendship and solidarity with the peace- and justice-loving peoples throughout the world, support the national liberation movements in Asia, Africa and Latin America, support all movements for peace, democracy and social progress in the world.

The above-mentioned political objective and twelve-point policy fully conform with the Laotian people's aspirations and ensure the interests of the nation and all nationalities and the Laotian people of all strata.

The Laotian Patriotic Front calls on all cadres and personnel in various branches, all armymen, the people of all social strata and nationalities, and all those who love their country and peace to further strengthen their unity and wage a resolute struggle to force the U.S. imperialists to end all acts of intervention against Laos, withdraw all their military advisers and personnel and all weapons and war means from Laos, and let the Laotian people live in peace and build their country in peace, independence, neutrality, democracy and prosperity.

So long as the U.S. imperialists and their lackeys in Laos persist in their scheme to conquer this country and betray the Laotians' interests, sabotage the peace, independence, neutrality, democracy and unity of this country, and obstruct the realization of the above-said goal and policy on the whole territory of Laos, the entire Laotian people will have to further strengthen the national united bloc and make all-out efforts to build and consolidate the liberated zone, turning it into a still firmer prop for the struggle to foil all the dark schemes of the enemy and win complete victory.

The Laotian Patriotic Front calls on the peace- and justive-loving peoples and governments all over the world to support the just struggle of the Laotian people and take appropriate measures to check the U.S. imperialists' intervention and aggression against Laos, and force them to let the internal affairs of Laos be settled by the Laotians themselves.

The just struggle of the Laotian people, enjoying warm sympathy and support from the peace- and justice-loving peoples throughout the world, is bound to win.

Let the entire people of Laos unite millions as one man. Let them fight resolutely against the U.S. aggressors, to save the country, and build a peaceful, independent, neutral, democratic, united, and prosperous Laos.

For many years now, the U.S. imperialists have carried out a policy of unceasing intervention and aggression in Laos in an attempt to turn it into a new-colony and a military base of the United States in South-East Asia.

In defiance of its obligations under the 1954 Geneva agreements and the 1962 Geneva agreements on Laos, the United States has trampled upon the independence and sovereignty and undermined the peace and neutrality of Laos. Over the past eight years, its intervention and aggression in Laos have grown ever more brazen. The United States, through a military putsch, has toppled the National Union Government which received investiture from the King and recognition from the 1962 Geneva agreements on Laos, and rigged up a stooge administration headed by Prince Souvanna Phouma and following a so-called policy of "peace and neutrality" by the agency of that administration, it has conducted a "special war" in Laos, it has launched bombing raids against the Laos territory, and used the Lao puppet army for repeated nibbling attacks on the areas under the control of the Lao Patriotic Forces.

True to the Lao people's aspirations for a peaceful, independent, neutral, democratic, unified and prosperous Laos, the Lao Patriot Front has always correctly implemented the 1962 Geneva agreements on Laos. In close alliance with the Lao Patriotic Neutralist Forces, it has exercised along with the people its legitimate right of self-defense, it has resolutely fought against the U.S. "special war"; it has opposed the nibbling attacks of the American and their stooges; it has inflicted on them fitting blows, and has recorded increasing victories.

While fighting against the U.S. intervention and aggression, the Lao Patriotic Front has repeatedly demonstrated its good will with regard to a peaceful settlement of the Lao problem. Its 12-point political programme and the maintenance of its representation in Vientiane are clear evidence of this good will.

Yet the United States and the Vientiane administration have ignored all reasonable and logical proposals made by the Lao Patriotic Front. Since, notably Nixon took office as President of the United States, the United States has intensified the war in Laos with even greater obstination.

The United States has brought more U.S. and Thailand military personnel, weapons and war materiel into Laos; it has strengthened the puppet army and the "special forces" under Vang Pao's command; it has launched repeated nibbling attacks against many places controlled by the patriotic [forces] from

131

the north to the south of the country. It has also put in action a modern airforce for saturation bombings against the territory of Laos, thus perpetrating extremely barbarous crimes against the Lao people.

Beginning August 1969 it mustered about 50 battalions of puppet troops and Thailand mercenaries, conducted operation "Kukiet" to nibble at the Plain of Jars-Xieng Khouang area. Meanwhile, it launched several nibbling operations against the liberated zone in central and southern Laos. What is particularly serious, since February 17, 1970, the United States has used B52 and planes of the type for mass bombings against the Plain of Jars-Xieng Khouang area, as well as against central and southern Laos, destroying hundreds of villages and savagely massacring the civilian population.

But the armed forces and people, resolved to defend the liberated areas, have smashed the nibbling attack of the United States and its agents in the Plain of Jars-Xieng Khouang area as well as other places. They have wiped out an important part of the U.S. commanded and fostered "special forces" and dealt a heavy blow at the "prestige" of the U.S. Air Force.

To cover up the Nixon administration's "escalation" of the war in Laos, the United States and the Vientiane administration have launched a campaign of slander against the Lao Patriotic Front and the Democratic Republic of Vietnam. At the same time, they have resorted to deceitful allegations about "peace" in an attempt to fool U.S. and world public opinion which is condemning the Nixon war of aggression in Laos.

The Nixon administration's attempt to "escalate" the aggressive war has brought about the present tension in Laos, and poses an extremely serious threat to peace and security in Indochina and South-East Asia.

In face of the tension in Laos, the Lao Patriotic Front affirms the necessity of ending the U.S. war and finding a political solution to the Lao problem.

The position of the Lao Patriotic Front is: The peaceful settlement of the Lao problem must be based on the 1962 Geneva agreements on Laos and on the actual situation in Laos. In more concrete terms:

1. All countries respect the sovereignty, independence, neutrality, unity and territorial integrity of the Kingdom of Laos, as provided for in the 1962 Geneva agreements on Laos. The United States must put an end to its intervention and aggression in Laos, stop escalating the war, completely cease the bombing of the Lao territory, withdraw from Laos all U.S. advisers and military personnel as well as all U.S. weapons and war material, stop using military bases in Thailand and Thailand mercenaries for purposes of aggression against Laos. It must stop using Lao territory for intervention and aggression against other countries.

2. In accordance with the 1962 Geneva agreements, the Kingdom of Laos refrains from joining any military alliance with foreign countries, and from allowing foreign countries to establish military bases in Laos and to introduce troops and military personnel into its territory.

The Kingdom of Laos follows a foreign policy of peace and neutrality, establishes relations with other countries in accordance with the five principles of peaceful coexistence, and accepts aid with no political conditions attached from all countries. With the other Indochinese countries, it establishes friendly and good-neighbour relations on the basis of the five principles of peaceful coexistence and of the principles of the 1954 Geneva agreements on Indochina and the 1962 Geneva agreements on Laos.

With regard to the Democratic Republic of Vietnam and the Republic of South Vietnam, it respects Vietnam's independence, sovereignty, unity and territorial integrity. With regard to the Kingdom of Cambodia, it respects the latter's independence, sovereignty, neutrality and territorial integrity within its present borders.

3. To respect the throne, to hold free and democratic general elections, to elect a national assembly and to set up a democratic government of national union truly representative of the Lao people of all nationalities, to build a peaceful, independent, neutral, democratic, unified, and prosperous Laos.

4. During the period from the restoration of peace to the general elections for setting up the national assembly, the parties concerned shall, in a spirit of national concord, equality and mutual respect, hold a consultative political conference composed of representatives of all Lao parties concerned in order to deal with all the affairs of Laos, and set up a provisional coalition government. The parties shall reach agreement on the establishment of a security zone to ensure the normal functioning of the consultative political conference and the provisional coalition government, free from all attempts at sabotage or pressure by forces from inside or outside Laos.

5. The unification of Laos shall be achieved through consultations between the Lao parties on the principle of equality and national concord. Pending this unification, no party shall use force to encroach upon or nibble at the areas controlled by another. The pro-American forces must withdraw forthwith from the areas they have illegally occupied, and resettle in their native places those people who have been forcibly removed from there. At the same time, they must pay compensations for damages caused to them. Each party pledges itself to refrain from discrimination and reprisals against those who have collaborated with another party.

The above-mentioned position of the Lao Patriotic Front for the settlement of the Lao problem meets the Lao people's earnest aspirations and is consistent with the interests of peace and security in Indochina, South-East Asia and the world. It is the just basis of a solution to the Lao problem.

The Lao problem must be settled among the Lao parties concerned. To create conditions for the Lao parties concerned to meet, the United States must, as an immediate step, stop escalating the war, and stop completely the bombing of Lao territory without posing any condition.

The Lao people deeply aspire for independence, freedom and peace. If the United States obdurately persists in its aggressive schemes, the Lao Patriotic Front, the Lao Patriotic Neutralist Forces and the Lao people are resolved to fight on till total victory.

The Lao Patriotic Front earnestly calls on the Lao people of all nationalities to closely unite around the military alliance between the Lao Patriotic Front and the Lao Patriotic Neutralist Forces, to heighten their vigilance, to stand ready and resolved to smash all military plans and deceitful schemes of the United States and its agents with a view to defending the liberated zone, safeguarding their fundamental national rights and contributing to the preservation of peace in Indochina and South-East Asia.

The Lao Patriotic Front instantly calls on the peace-and justice-loving governments, the American people and the world's peoples strongly support the Lao people's just struggle, and resolutely demand that the United States stop its war of aggression in Laos and, as an immediate step, put a complete end to the bombing of Lao territory.

With the broad sympathy and strong support of the world's peoples, the entire Lao people, closely united, are sure to defeat the U.S. aggressors and their agents, and successfully build a peaceful, independent, neutral, democratic unified and prosperous Laos.

Appendix F: Agreement on the Restoration of Peace and Reconciliation in Laos (Unofficial Translation)

In response to the august desire of His Majesty the King and the earnest hope of the entire Lao people who wish to end the war soon, to restore and preserve a durable peace, and to achieve national reconciliation to unify the nation, to make Laos a peaceful country and establish its independence, neutrality, democracy and prosperity so it may play a role in the development of peace in Indochina and Southeast Asia, based on the 1962 Geneva Agreement concerning Laos and the current situation in Laos, the Vientiane Government side and the Patriotic Forces side have agreed unanimously as follows:

Part I
General Principles
Article 1

(a) The intention of the Lao people is to firmly preserve and resolutely apply basic and inviolable national rights, such as the independence, sovereignty, unity and territorial integrity of Laos.

(b) The declaration on the neutrality of Laos, dated July 9, 1962, and the 1962 Geneva Agreements on Laos are the correct bases for the peaceful, independent and neutral foreign policy for the Kingdom of Laos; the Lao parties concerned, the United States, Thailand and other foreign states must scrupulously respect and apply them. The internal problems of Laos must be solved by the Lao people themselves without foreign interference.

(c) Given the noble goal to restore peace, consolidate independence, achieve national reconciliation and unite the nation, and given the present situation in Laos, in which there are two zones and two separate Administrations, the Lao internal problem must be solved in accordance with the spirit of national reconciliation, based on the principle of equality and mutual respect without either side pressuring or annexing the other.

(d) To preserve national independence and sovereignty, promote national reconciliation and unite the country, it is necessary to carefully observe the rights and freedoms of the people, such as: individual liberty, freedom of religion, freedom of speech, freedom of the press, freedom of assembly, freedom to form political parties and associations, freedom to vote and to run for office, freedom of travel, freedom to residence, freedom of trade, and freedom to own personal property; all laws, regulations and organizations prohibiting the above-mentioned rights must be abolished.

Part II
Articles Concerning Military Affairs
Article 2

At 1200 noon on February 22, 1973, Vientiane time, a ceasefire-in-place will be carried out fully and simultaneously throughout Laos, including the following:

(a) foreign countries will cease completely and permanently the bombing of all Lao territory, will cease intervention and aggression in Laos, and will cease all military involvement in Laos.

(b) all foreign armed forces will completely and permanently cease all military activities in Laos.

(c) all armed forces of all Lao factions will cease completely all military activities that constitute hostilities toward one another, both on the ground and in the air.

Article 3

Following the ceasefire:

(a) ground or air forces are forbidden all activities to attack, annex, threaten and enter territory temporarily under the control of the other side.

(b) all military actions which constitute other hostile acts are forbidden, including banditry, suppression, armed activity, and espionage by air and ground means. If one side wishes to resupply its own side with foodstuffs by passing through the zone of the other side, the Committee to implement the Agreement will consult and agree on establishing specific measures for this.

(c) All "sweep" operations, terrorism and suppression which endanger the lives and property of the people, as well as acts of revenge and discrimination against people who have cooperated with the opposite side during the war, are forbidden: to help the people who were forced to flee from their homes during the war to be free to return and earn a living according to their wishes.

(d) It is forbidden to bring into Laos all types of military personnel, regular troops and irregular troops of all kinds and all kinds of foreign-made weapons or war material, except for those specified in the Geneva Agreements of 1954 and 1962. In case it is necessary to replace damaged or worn-out weapons or war materials, both sides will consult and arrive at an agreement.

Article 4

Within a period no longer than 60 days, counting from the date of establishment of the Provisional Government and the Joint National Political Council, the withdrawal of foreign military personnel, regular and irregular, from Laos, and the dismantling of foreign military and paramilitary organizations must be totally completed. "Special Forces"—organized, trained, equipped and controlled by foreigners—must be disbanded; all bases, military installations and positions of these forces must be liquidated.

Article 5

Both Lao sides will return to each other all persons regardless of nationality that were captured, and those imprisoned for cooperating with the other side, during the war. Their return will be carried out according to the procedures set up by the two sides, and, at the latest, must be completed within 60 days following the establishment of the Provisional Government of National Union and the Joint National Political Council.

After all those who were captured have been returned, each side has the duty to gather information on those missing during the war and report the information to the other side.

Part III
Articles Concerning Politics
Article 6

General elections shall be held in accordance with the principles of freedom and democracy in order to elect a National Assembly and establish a Government of National Union, which will truly represent all the people of all nationalities throughout Laos. The procedures and the timing for the elections will be agreed between the two sides.

Before these elections are held, and not later than 30 days after the signing of this Agreement, the two sides will establish a Provisional Government of National Union and a Joint National Political Council, to carry out the Agreements which have been signed and to administer the affairs of the nation.

Article 7

The new Provisional Government of National Union will consist of representatives of the Vientiane Government side and of the Patriotic Forces side in equal number, and two qualified persons who are for peace, independence, neutrality and democracy, as agreed upon by the two sides. The Prime Minister-to-be will be outside the equal apportionment to the two sides. The Provisional Government of National Union will be set up under a special procedure with the agreement of the King: it will work according to the principle of unanimity between the two sides. It will have the duty of carrying out the agreements signed and the political programs which the two sides have agreed to, for instance, the carrying out of the ceasefire, the preservation of a durable peace, to implement in full the democratic rights of the people, to practice a peaceful, independent and neutral foreign policy, to coordinate plans for economic development, cultural expansion, and to receive and distribute combined foreign assistance from various countries aiding Laos.

Article 8

The Joint National Political Council is an organization of national reconciliation, consisting of equal numbers of representatives of the Vientiane Government side and the Patriotic Forces side, as well as other qualified persons who support peace, independence, neutrality and democracy in a number to be agreed on by both sides, working in accordance with the principle of unanimity in consultations between both sides and having the following duties.

—consult and furnish opinions to the Provisional Government of National Union on major questions of domestic and foreign affairs of the nation.
—support and assist the provisional Government of National Union and the two sides in implementing the Agreement, in order to successfully achieve national reconciliation.
—examine and agree together with the Provisional Government of National Union on laws and regulations relating to general elections and to cooperate with the Provisional Government of National Union in setting up the elections to elect a National Assembly and to set up a regular National Government.

The procedure for establishing the Joint National Political Council is as follows: both sides will discuss the subject in detail and come to a decision which they will forward to the Provisional Government of National Union to be submitted to the King for the final appointment. The same procedure will be followed to effect the dissolution of the Council.

Article 9

The two sides agree to neutralize Luang Prabang and Vientiane and to seek every method to guarantee the security of the Provisional Government of National

Union and the Joint National Political Council and their effective functioning and to protect them from sabotage or pressure from any force within or without.

Article 10

(a) While awaiting the election of the National Assembly and the establishment of the Permanent Government of National Union, in accordance with the spirit of Article 6 of Part II of the Joint Communique issued at Zurich June 22, 1961, both sides will preserve their own zones of temporary control and will attempt to carry out the political programs of the Provisional Government of National Union which the two sides have agreed upon.

(b) Both sides will promote normal relations between the two zones, setting up favorable conditions for the people to travel, earn a living, visit one another, carry out economic, cultural and other exchanges and other activities in order to develop national concord and build national unity quickly.

(c) Both sides take cognizance of the announcement of the American Government that it will participate in healing the wounds of the war and in the reconstruction of Indochina after the war. The Government of National Union will discuss with the American Government such participation in regards to Laos.

Part IV

Concerning the Joint Commission to Implement the Agreement and the International Commission for Supervision and Control.

Article 11

The implementation of this Agreement is primarily the responsibility of the two sides concerned in Laos. The two sides will immediately set up a Commission to implement the Agreement with an equal number of representatives from each side. The Commission to implement the Agreement will begin to function immediately after the ceasefire is effective. The Commission to implement the Agreement will function according to the principle of unanimity in consultation.

Article 12

The International Commission for Supervision and Control, which was set up according to the 1962 Geneva Agreement on Laos, consisting of representatives of India, Poland and Canada, with India being the Chairman, will continue its activity in accordance with the duties, powers, and working principles stipulated in the Protocol of the above-mentioned Agreements.

Part V
Other Dispositions
Article 13

The Vientiane Government side and the Patriotic Forces side promise to carry out this Agreement and to pursue negotiations to bring to reality all the provisions that they have agreed to and to solve the remaining problem involving the two sides. in a spirit of equality and mutual respect in order to put an end to the war, restore and preserve a durable peace, carry out reconciliation, build national unity and lead the nation to become peaceful, independent, neutral, democratic, unified and prosperous.

Article 14

The present Agreement is effective as of the date of signing. Done at Vientiane, February 21, 1973, in five copies in Lao:

   —one copy for H.M. The King;
   —one copy for each side;
   —one copy for the archives of the Provisional Government of National Union; and
   —one copy for the archives of the Joint National Political Council.

Representative of the
Vientiane Government

Phagna Pheng Phongsavan,
Special Plenipotentiary
Representative of the
Vientiane Government

Representative of the Party
of the Patriotic Forces

Phagna Phoumi Vongvichit,
Special Plenipotentiary
Representative of the
Patriotic Forces

Appendix G: Front Groups and Mass Organizations

The following is a sample of groups and organizations that comprise the Lao Patriotic Front. The list has been compiled from a variety of sources, including working lists of U.S. government officials, Pathet Lao radio broadcasts, and Pathet Lao publications. Except for notations of FBIS or *Voix du Laos* translations of PL radio broadcasts, no attempt has been made to document the mention of these organizations. There are undoubtedly inaccuracies in this list, and it certainly does not include all Neo Lao Hak Sat organizations. The list is given here to provide examples of NLHS organizational effort.

Front Groups

Dissident Neutralists

Buddhist Associations

Neo Hom Heng Sat, reported in 1957 in Houa Phan Province; replaced by broader front. Presently known as Association of Bonzes, United Buddhist Organization, or Buddhist Amity Association. Centered in Xieng Khouang; Phra Bouakham Vorapet and Phra Khathanh Thempbouri are leaders.
Religious Amity (Sasana Samphan)
Laotian Buddhist Association, since 1963 (FBIS to at least 1967)

Labor Organizations

Two formed in early 1960s: Lao Workers' Union and Phou Pakob Asip (Lao Workers' Association)
Laotian Employees Federation (FBIS 8-14-64; 8-30-66)
Laotian Patriotic Trade Unions Committee (FBIS 6-3-69)
Printing Workers of NLHS Central Committee (*Voix du Laos*, May 4, 1965; 2-15-67)

Federation of Civil Servants

Appearance of this group first noted in October 1963; apparently includes all NLHS and Deuanists.

Civil Servants' Federation (Sahaphan Kharatsakan—may not be exact Lao term)

Civic Servants' Union (FBIS 7-24-69)

Laotian Public Servants Association (FBIS 6-3-65; 8-18-66)

Federation of Laotian Government Functionaries (FBIS 6-24-64; 9-23-63; 8-17-66)

National Youth Federation

Set up in November 1961 during NLHS alliance with Kong Le; may be assumed to have been dissolved at the time of the fighting between Kong Le and NLHS or, if not, Deuanists replaced Kong Le faction.

Laotian Youth Federation, Nouphan Sitphasay, president (FBIS 3-4-69; Peking, 6-64)

Mitaphab (Club for Lao Students from Abroad)

Formed in October 1961, originally based in Khang Khay; at first followed the Santiphab party, but by mid-1963 the majority was more pro-NLHS. Publishes paper *Mitaphab* in Lao and French, about 300 weekly distribution.

Laotian Students Friendship Association (*Voix du Laos*, 3-15-64; 5-18-65)

Committee for Peace, Neutrality, and Reconciliation

Founded November 1960 by Mitaphab, Santiphab, NLHS, and Kong Le groups; 1961 Central Committee included several PPL members; Committee for the Construction of Peace, Neutrality, and National Harmony and Unification.

National Committee of Struggle Against U.S. Imperialism and in Support of the South Vietnamese People

Formed in Khang Khay, mid-December 1963, at joint meeting of mass organizations, fronts, and political parties organized by Committee for Peace, Neutrality, and Reconciliation; chaired by Nouhak with Deuane as vice-chairman; included almost every prominent NLHS and Deuanist name.

*Laotian Afro-Asian People's Solidarity
Committee* (FBIS, 3-4-69)

Patriotic Teachers' Association (FBIS, 7-24-69)

NLHS Cultural Association (FBIS, 4-27-66)

Formed April 1966.
Laotian Patriotic Cultural Workers Association (FBIS, Hanoi, 3-14-67)

Laotian Graduate Students Association
(FBIS, Peking, 8-5-66)

*Association in Support of Laotian Peace
and Neutralism* (students) (FBIS, 10-19-65; 9-20-63)

Mass Organizations

Samakhom

Men's, women's, and youths' organizations in villages; includes virtually all villagers; openly NLHS.

Samakhom Mening Lao or Samakham Sati: Lao Women's Association. Existed in some form since Viet Minh-Pathet Lao offensive in 1953; Pathet Lao Women's Association was predecessor, formed in Houa Phan in 1953, led by wives of Souphanouvong, Phoumi Vongvichit, Kaysone, and (Phya) Hom Sombat; probably also called Youvannary instead of Pathet Lao Women's Association.

Present Lao Women's Association founded in August 1962, in Xieng Khouang; top-level reorganization of mass women's organization.

Laotian Patriotic Women's Union, Mme. Khamphong Boupha, president (FBIS, 2-14-69)

Laotian Women's Union, Mme. Phay Boun Pholsena, president (FBIS, 2-25-69)

Samakhom Sao Hay Na (men's): Association of Peasants aka People's Association, aka Farmers' Association, aka Samakhom Lao Hak Sat, Farmers' Association (Samakhom Sao Hay Na may not be exact Lao term).

Samakhom Sao Noum (youths'). From mid-teens to thirty years of age or marriage; Ongkan Saonoum.

Samakhom Lao Noum Hak Sat: Organization for Patriotic Youth; may be only for potential cadres rather than true mass organization; men seventeen to thirty; girls sixteen to twenty-five.

Association of Lao Patriotic Youth (Samakhom Lao Noum Hak Sat)

Young Women's Organization (Ongkan Nyouvannary).

Laotian Patriotic Youth Union (FBIS, 2-14-69); (same as Samakhom Lao Noum Hak Sat?)

Organization of Militant Youth (Ongkan Saonoum Jomti).

Appendix H: Selective List of Persons Interviewed or Consulted

A. **Lao Who at One Time or Another Were with the Pathet Lao**
(including Lao Loum as well as persons of Meo, Lao Theung, Black Tai, and other Tai descent)

1. Defector; b. 1944, Luang Prabang Prov; Meo
   Ed: primary, ages 9 to 10½
   Occ before joining: farmer
   PL service: 1957-Jul 1959, in PL village unit, sgt; Feb 1960-Mar 1967—Lt, asst chief QM office in KKhay
   NVN trng; mil admin course Nov 1961 for 30 mos
   Def: Mar 1967

2. Defector; b. 1940, Nong Khai, Thailand; Tai
   Ed: med trng, course at OB hosp, Vientiane; studied in Vientiane wat (about ages 15 to 19)
   Occ before joining: supply clk at OB hosp
   PL service: 1962-1966; 1962—joined Kong Le, briefly arrested by PL, given med trng & worked in villages for Kong Le Neutralists; 1963—captured by PL & Deuane Neutralists, then coolie & nurse in KKhay
   Def: Aug 1966

3. Defector; b. 1930, Sayaboury
   Ed: no formal ed
   PL service: 1954-1957, soldier; 1959—fled into jungle & stayed there as guerrilla; 1960—joined Kong Le forces; 1962-66—PL forces, 2nd Lt; 1963—asst co cmdr
   Def: Sep 1966

4. Defector; b. 1931, Khammouane Prov; Tai Dam (moved with family to SVN in 1937)
   Ed: ages 6 to 18, in SVN
   Occ before joining: 1949-1953—served in French Army until captured by VM; 1955-1957—prisoner in NVN; 1957-1962—released and served in NVA (squad ldr, taught mil subjects to Lao, interpreter at Son Tay)
   PL service: 1962-1966, cmdr of Lao 2nd Co under NVA 36th Bn; later, asst co cmdr in PL bn in Saravane
   Def: Jun 1966

5. Defector; b. Jun 1937, Xieng Khouang Prov

Ed: learned to read & write Lao at local temple

Occ before joining: farmer

PL service: 1953-57, sgt & chief cook in PL bn; 1961-63—mil pol with Kong Le faction until captured by PL; 1963-67—S/Lt & propagandist

Def: Feb 6, 1967

6. Prisoner; b. 1946, Sedone Prov

Ed: 2 yrs (1957-59)

Occ before joining: student

PL service: 1959-1966 or 1967; 1966—chief of QM with regional hq at Lao Ngam

Cap: 1966 or 1967

7. Defector; b. about 1948, Luang Prabang Prov

Ed: 3 mos primary sch; can read & write; med trng for 7 mos under PL

PL service: 1961-1967; in dance show for propag purposes; 1964—Nam The hosp where she met Ngo Van Dam (see B-10) in late 1966

Def: May 1967

8. Defector; b. 1938, Luang Prabang Prov

Ed: can read & write

Occ before joining: farmer

PL service: 1960-1966, soldier & propagandist

Def: Sep 1966

9. At present high police official, Pakse; b. 1930, Sedone Prov

Occ before joining: schoolteacher

PL service: 1950-1955, cadet sch; Co Cmdr; 1953—to VN; 1954—C/S of southern Laos, representative of Lao Issara in Central Commission & member of Mixed Sub-Commission in Paksong; member of PPL

Def: Oct 1955

10. Defector; b. 1938, Attopeu Prov

Ed: 3 yrs as novice monk until age 21

Occ before joining: student

PL service and NVN trng: 1959-1966; 1959-1964—med student in Ha Dong; chief of med unit in Attopeu after 1964 grad; capt.

Def: Sep 1966

11. Prisoner; b. 1930, Khammouane Prov

Ed: 2 yrs formal, 3 mos French Army trng (1944)

Occ before joining: farmer, then volunt'd for French Army (1951-53)

PL service: 1953—fled to VN, worked as cook to wealthy Lao, then sent to Savannakhet Prov as warehouse keeper for PL; 1956—PL driver; 1958—demob'd; 1960-1966—Kong Le driver & laborer in tool shop for PL

NVN trng: 1955—mechanic

Cap: May 1967

12. Defector; b. Attopeu Prov

   Ed: learned to read & write in war

   PL service: 1954-1957, soldier in inf unit; 1957-1959—sent home, farmer; 1959-1967—M/Sgt, asst cmdr, 1st Lt of Ind Co; 1966—assigned to regional hq in Savannakhet Prov

   NVN trng: 1954—post-Geneva; 1955—6 mos at Muong Vinh

   Def: Spring 1967

13. Defector; b. 1937, Khammouane Prov

   Ed: taught self to read & write; 1955-1958—novice monk (2½ yrs)

   Occ before joining: farmer

   PL service: 1959-1967—propagandist, Lt

   Def: Apr 1967

14. At present in Min of Info, RLG; b. Dec 1931, near Tchepone

   Ed: sch in Savannakhet, Pakse, & Vientiane

   Occ before joining: student

   PL service: 1945-1957, Issara guard under Thao O; 1946—moved with unit to VN; next few years, into Laos for propag work; 1948—head of polit section in Exec Cmte for Nat'l Liberation organized in VN

   NVN trng: 1954-1957; 1952—propag chief of subdiv in Mahaxay; on ed staff of *Neo Lao Hak Sat* newspaper

15. Defector; b. 1941, Savannakhet Prov; Lao Theung

   PL service: 1957-Jan 1967; 1958—propagandist; asst plat ldr, 2nd Lt

   NVN trng: 1958 (3 mos); 1959 (5 mos)

   Def: Jan 1967

16. Defector; b. 1927, Luang Prabang Prov

   Ed: literate

   PL service: 1953-1964; 1953—appt'd canton chief by VM; 1957—worked in devl section of LPrabang Prov cmte; 1963—named dist chief of Pakseng until 1964, when asked to resign; then a farmer

   Def: Feb 1967

17. Defector; b. 1939, Luang Prabang Prov

   Ed: to elem grade 4

   Occ before joining: student

   PL service: 1959-1966; 1965—chief of QM unit, LPrabang region

   NVN trng: 1959 (3 mos); 1963—cadet sch near Hanoi; 1½ yrs polit, mil, and QM courses

   Def: Aug 1966

18. At present RLG Lt Col; b. about 1925, Savannakhet Prov

   Occ before joining: in father's opium business

   PL service: 1946-1957

   NVN trng: 1946-48; 1951—member of mil cmte for Sam Neua Prov; 1955—Director of Khommadam Sch for off trng; then directed guerrilla troops in SNeua & PSaly; rank of major when he rallied to RLG in 1957

19. Defector

    PL service: 1945-49 & 1952-56; dir of off sch, med sch, & QM of Xieng Khouang area

    Def: 1956

20. Defector; b. 1942, Luang Prabang Prov

    Ed: elem until age 12

    Occ before joining: student

    PL service: Oct 1954-Jan 1967; 1962—capt & co cmdr; 1964—cmdr of protection co with Souk Vongsak in Vientiane

    NVN trng: 1955—DBPhu (6 mos); 1957—adv trng (18 mos); 1961—Son Tay, adv trng (10 mos)

    Def: Jan 1967

21. Defector

    Ed: grade 2 (French system)

    Occ before joining: student PL service: 1952-Sep 1965, bodyguard, medic; 1960—co cmdr; 1962—mil staff member, Attopeu Region; Lt cmdr, Sithandone; Dec 1964—chief of combat section under Gen Phomma

    NVN trng: 1953-55; 1958-59 (1 yr 2 mos) medical course; 1960-61—Dong Hoi (8 mos adv trng)

    Def: Sep 1965

22. Defector; b. 1936 or 1937, Sedone Prov

    Ed: 1 yr in monk's sch for elem ed; 4 yrs monk trng in Thailand (1947-51)

    Occ before joining: student monk

    PL service: 1954-67, C/S 2nd PL prov bn

    NVN trng: 1954-57, automechanics at Bac Yang (3 yrs); about 1959—at Son Tay for off trng, graduated as capt & co cmdr

    Def: Feb 1967

23. Defector; b. 1940, Sam Neua Prov

    Ed: 6 yrs from ages 12 to 18; also teacher trng course in Sam Neua

    Occ before joining: trader in clothes and opium (3 yrs)

    PL service: Nov 1960 to 1966—PL teacher, with ed dept in Sam Neua, sch director in Sam Neua

    Def: 1966

24. At present official in RLG judiciary, Savannakhet; b. 1919, Tchepone

    Ed: Savannakhet (1928-31); Hanoi (l'Ecole des Frères and Institut Gia Long, 1931-37)

    Occ before joining: commerce; with French company operating a lead mine near Tchepone as liaison agent

    PL service: 1945-57; 1945—chosen cmdr of Issara forces of Tchepone; 1946-49—to VN to organize forces and direct guerrilla and propag forces in Laos; formed Cmte for Nat'l Liberation with Nouhak as chief, while maintaining liaison with Issara govt in Thailand; 1949-57—returned to Laos to command local troops in Tchepone; from there to NVN, where interned with family (about 3 yrs); then served in minor functions, including liaison to ICC, until his integration into RLG in 1957

25. Defector; b. 1935, Vientiane Prov
    Ed: elem
    Occ before joining: 1960-63, in Kong Le's Neutralist police until taken prisoner by PL
    PL service: 1963-65, warrant officer; 1964—policeman in KKhay; Apr—1965—polit instructor to ex-RLG personnel in Deuane forces
    Def: Dec 1965

26. Defector; b. probably late 1940s, Sam Neua Prov
    Ed: can read & write
    Occ before joining: farmer
    PL service: 1960-66, soldier & propagandist
    Def: Sep 1966

27. Defector; middle-aged; b. near Muong Hong, NE Laos; Meo
    Ed: cannot read or write
    Occ before joining: farmer, asst village chief (1954-58), Xieng Ngeun
    PL service: 1958-66, propag agent near native village
    NVN trng: 1961-62, Hanoi & Haiphong
    Def: Oct 1966

28. Defector; b. 1940, Xieng Khouang Prov
    Ed: grade 6, elem
    Occ before joining: teacher
    PL service: 1962-66; 1962—village captured by PL, served as PL instructor
    Def: Sep 1966

29. Defector; b. 1929, Saravane Prov; Lao Theung
    Ed: learned to read & write in wat; novice monk (3 yrs)
    Occ before joining: farmer
    PL service: 1950-54, propagandist; 1960-66—soldier
    Def: 1966

30. Defector; b. 1921, Khammouane Prov
    Ed: self-educated, reads & writes Lao
    Occ before joining: farmer, after being RLG asst platoon ldr of home guards
    PL service: 1962-66, PL canton chief
    Def: Nov 1966

31. Defector; b. Sep 1942, Sedone Prov
    Ed: 1948-61; attended Collège of Pakse and spent 4 mos at wat as novice monk

Occ before joining: student

PL service: 1961-66, mechanic & asst platoon ldr; 1963–S/Lt

NVN trng: 1961-63, Dong Hoi and Thai Nguyen Tech Sch, auto-
mechanics

Def: Dec 1966

B. Members of North Vietnamese Army (NVA) in Laos

1. Defector; b. 1946, Thanh Hoa, NVN; Tai Dam

   Ed: 6 yrs village sch

   Occ before joining: farmer

   NVA service: Apr 1963-Mar 1967; 1964–to Laos as soldier; 1965–
   made cpl & stationed at Muong Sa, Laos; 1966–2nd Lt, asst co
   cmdr, Bn 923, Laos; 1967–in Houei Tom attack when defected

   Def: Mar 1967

2. Prisoner; b. 1943, NW NVN; Chinese-Tai Dam

   Ed: 5th class, DRV

   Occ before joining: oxcart driver in cooperative

   NVA service: Jul 1966-Jan 1967, private; Jan 1967–to Laos, taken
   while attacking FAR post

   Cap: Jan 1967

3. Prisoner; b. 1947, Yen Bai, NVN; Vietnamese

   Ed: about 3 yrs

   Occ before joining: farmer

   NVA service: 1966-Jan 1967, soldier; Oct 1966–to Laos; Jan
   1967–wounded and taken in attack by FAR

   Cap: Jan 1967

4. Defector; b. 1943, Xieng Khouang Prov, Laos; Tai Deng (Red Tai);
   moved with family to VN in 1951 (move forced by VN troops)

   NVA service: 1959-66; orderly to VN adviser in Xieng Khouang Prov,
   Laos, & also with VN adviser to 17th PL Bn, Khammouane Prov;
   propagandist & soldier in Thakhek area until defection

   Def: Jul 1966

5. Prisoner; b. 1946, NVN; Vietnamese NVA service: 1965-Feb 1966,
   solider; Jan 1966–to Laos, wounded and taken prisoner

   Cap: Feb 1966

6. Defector; b. 1945, Vientiane Prov; Vietnamese

   Ed: speaks, reads, writes Thai & Vietnamese (moved with family to
   Thailand 1945-62); also 10 mos mech trng Phu Tho, NVN

   Occ before joining: mechanics student

   NVA service: 1962–recruited by VN agents in Thailand & sent to NVN;
   1965–recruited into NVA; 1965–assigned to SVN; defected while
   going through Laos

Def: Apr 1966

7. Prisoner; b. 1930, Nghe An, NVN; Vietnamese
   NVA service: capt; 1965—arr in Laos, fought in Thakhek battle
   Cap: Nov 1965

8. Defector; b. 1942, Muong Lan, NVN; Vietnamese-Tai Dam
   NVA service: 1962-66; 1965—squad ldr & jr off after grad from cadet
     sch, Thanh Hoa; Sep 1965—to Laos
   Def: Dec 1966

9. Defector; b. Dec 1930, Thanh Hoa, NVN; Vietnamese
   NVA service: Jan 1950-Dec 1966; 1958-60—off sch at Son Tay &
     promoted to 1st Lt; 1963—acted as C/S to Bn 1; Feb 1964—to Laos
     as adviser to PL Bn 408; Oct 1966—Sr Capt
   Def: Dec 1966

10. Defector
    Occ before joining: med student finishing 1st yr of 5 yr course at Ha
      Dong NVA service: Oct 1966-May 1967; Oct 1966—to Laos to head
      Nam Tha Prov med services for VNese and to advise PL
    Def: May 1967

11. Prisoner; b. 1942, Vinh Phuc Prov, NVN; Vietnamese
    Ed: completed 5th grade
    Occ before joining: farmer (1960-64)
    NVA service: 1964-Jul 1966, soldier; May 1966—to Laos
    Cap: Jul 1966

12. Defector; b. 1937, Thanh Hoa, NVN
    Ed: 3 yrs (1952-55)
    NVA service: 1959-67, S/Lt, subaltern in QM service; May 1964—to
      Laos, Attopeu Prov; Feb 1965—polit agt for VNese with PL
    Married: Mar 1966
    Def: Apr 1967

13. Prisoner; b. 1949, NW NVN; Vietnamese
    Ed: 5 yrs (1960-65)
    NVA service: Jan 1966-Mar 1967, private; Jul 1966—to Laos, in combat
      about 5 days after trng about 6 mos
    Cap: Mar 1967

14. Prisoner; b. 1948; Vietnamese
    NVA service: 1966-Aug 1967; May 1967—intel recce mission to Laos in
      commando co when taken following NVA attack in Saravane on
      FAR post
    Cap: Aug 1967

15. Prisoner; Vietnamese
    NVA service: Aug-Sep 1966, soldier; Aug 1966—to Laos when wounded
      and taken prisoner
    Cap: Sep 1966

16. Prisoner; b. 1940; Vietnamese

Ed: 3rd grade

NVA service: 1963-65; assigned to 1st Ind Bn & then to Laos, cpl; in Thakhek battle

Cap: Nov 1965

17. Prisoner; b. 1946, NVN; Vietnamese

Ed: 4 yrs

NVA service: 1964-65; 1965—sent to Laos, wounded and taken at Dong Hene

Cap: Mar 1965

18. Prisoner; Vietnamese

NVA service: 1958-65, low-level comm off; 1965—arr Laos, in Thakhek attack

Cap: Nov 1965

19. Defector; b. NVN; Meo

Ed: no formal ed

NVA service: 1962-67, sgt; propagandist amg Meo in Laos

Def: after Tet 1967

20. Prisoner; b. 1947 (approx); Vietnamese

NVA service: 1964-65, soldier; Oct 1965—entered Laos and taken prisoner after wounded

Cap: Dec 1965

21. Defector; b. 1945, Nghe An Prov, NVN; Tai Dam

Ed: primary (1959-66)

NVA service: Jan-Feb 1967, private; assigned to road repair unit near Ban Ban, XKhouang, Laos

Def: Feb 1967

22. Defector; b. 1947, Xieng Khouang Prov; Lao Loum Ed: 1953-63, in Hanoi, thru 8th grade under govt sponsorship, grew up in orphanages

NVA service: 1964-67; Spring 1964—to Laos, aspirant, platoon ldr

Def: Jun 1967

Notes

Notes

Chapter 1
The Pathet Lao Leadership

1. Foreign Broadcast Information Service, (FBIS), July 15, 1969.

2. For an account of the Viet Minh's early relationships with these mountain minorities, see the article by John T. McAlister, Jr., in Peter Kunstadter, ed., SOUTHEAST ASIAN TRIBES, MINORITIES AND NATIONS (Princeton: Princeton University Press, 1966).

3. See Robert Scalapino, ed., THE COMMUNIST REVOLUTION IN ASIA, rev. ed. (Englewood Cliffs, N.J.: Prentice-Hall, 1969), Chapter 1.

4. See Paul F. Langer and Joseph J. Zasloff, NORTH VIETNAM AND THE PATHET LAO (Cambridge, Mass.: Harvard University Press, 1970), Chapter III.

Chapter 2
The People's Party of Laos

1. THIRTY YEARS OF STRUGGLE OF THE PARTY, Book I (Hanoi: Foreign Languages Publishing House, 1960), p. 26. This official DRV study was published to commemorate the thirtieth anniversay "of the founding of the Indochinese Communist Party, now the Vietnam Lao Dong Party."

2. Ibid., p. 23. For a fuller description of this factionalism, see Jean Lacouture, HO CHI MINH, A POLITICAL BIOGRAPHY (New York: Random House, 1968), pp. 53-60.

3. THIRTY YEARS OF STRUGGLE, p. 27.

4. See Lacouture, HO CHI MINH, p. 58, and Denis Duncanson, GOVERN-MENT AND REVOLUTION IN VIETNAM (New York: Oxford University Press, 1968), p. 144.

5. The DRV official study points out that at the time of the meeting that founded the party, there were in all 211 members, described as "Vietnamese Communists," in the following former factions: Indochinese Communist Party, 85; Annamese Communist Federation, 61; Indochinese Communist Federation, 11; and Vietnamese Communists in Hong Kong and abroad, 54. THIRTY YEARS OF STRUGGLE, p. 24.

6. Vietnam Central Information Service, MANIFESTO AND PLATFORMS OF THE VIETNAM LAO DONG PARTY (n.p., April 1952).

7. For example, see Bernard Fall, "The Pathet Lao," in Scalapino (ed.) THE COMMUNIST REVOLUTION IN ASIA, 1st edition.

8. See Paul F. Langer and Joseph J. Zasloff, NORTH VIETNAM AND THE PATHET LAO (Cambridge, Mass.: Harvard University Press, 1970), p. 96.

9. The sources include: a newly translated party training document (apparently widely used, since it has been found in printed and mimeographed form in several regions) containing questions and answers about the party (LP-24; LBN 10-14; and EMB-AP 11, dated July 30, 1960); an article, "Lumières sur l'origine du parti communiste au Laos," written by a former member of the Lao Communist movement, published in an RLG newspaper, XAT LAO, on December 20, 1968; and the notebook of a North Vietnamese economic cadre who served in Laos during 1968.

10. According to the XAT LAO account (December 20, 1968), Phoumi Vongvichit formed a party called SAHA SIB (vie commune); Mune organized the Peasant's party; and Khamtay Siphandone and Phoun Sipraseuth formed a group they called the Indochinese Communist party. Each had its Vietnamese advisers: Le Nhuy Huong, Vu Van Ke, Le Manh, and Chanh, respectively. We have not been able to find biographical information about the four advisers.

11. The XAT LAO article (December 20, 1968) states that Nouhak, Kaysone, Khamtay, Mune, Sisavath, Sisomphone, and Phoumi Vongvichit were called together by the Viet Minh advisers to form this party. When Phoumi Vongvichit objected, believing that the NLHS, or Lao Patriotic Front, was sufficient, Nouhak, Khamtay and Kaysone began secretly to organize, finally bringing Phoumi along with them.

12. A recent party document confirms the official establishment of the party on March 22, 1955, and applauds its predecessor, the Indochinese Communist party. This document, which reports the speech of the PPL secretary for Xieng Khouang Province, Da Thetthany, on March 22, 1969, "the 14th anniversay of the establishment of the PPL," contains the following passage:

During the fourteen-year period that has just ended, members of our PPL, who are people of the working class who revere the lessons of bravery and wisdom of the Indochinese Communist Party, have been loyal to the ideology of Marxism-Leninism. We have been adapting the general principles of Marxism-Leninism to the needs of Lao society, and this has enabled our party to successfully engineer the revolution in Laos in the face of all difficulties as well as to effect changes in Lao society.

13. The North Vietnamese economic cadre's notebook entry, labeling the 1957-1958 period a difficult one for the party, probably also reflects Hanoi's displeasure at the attempts of the NLHS to integrate with the RLG. As we have pointed out in our previous study, although North Vietnam did not attempt to sabotage the integration efforts, neither did it strongly support them, and it made preparations for their failure. See Langer and Zasloff, NORTH VIETNAM AND THE PATHET LAO, p. 65.

14. For a discussion of this offensive and its implications, see Langer and Zasloff, NORTH VIETNAM AND THE PATHET LAO, pp. 67-70; also A.M. Halpern and H.D. Fredman, COMMUNIST STRATEGY IN LAOS, RM-2561 (Santa Monica, Calif.: RAND Corporation, June 14, 1960), Chapter 5.

15. For an account of the Vietnamese Communist strategy of directing a "national united front" with a disciplined clandestine party, see P.J. Honey, "The National United Front in Vietnam," in STUDIES IN COMPARATIVE COMMUNISM, Vol. 2, No. 1 (January 1969), pp. 69-95. See also Hoang Van Chi, "Contribution to Development of a Rational Method for Identification of Political Parties and Organization," a paper presented at the international seminar on Communism in Asia sponsored by the Division of Communist Affairs, Asiatic Research Center, in Onyang, June 20-24, 1966.

16. The letter was sent on the occasion of the Japanese Communist party's tenth convention. It began, "Dear Fellow Comrades," and spoke of the NLHS and the PPL as separate entities, with the latter directing the former. It bore the notation, "October 24, 1966. At Sam Neua. Kaysone Phomvihan, Secretary General, representing the Central Committee of the People's Party of Laos." ZEN'EI (VANGUARD), December 1966.

On July 15, 1967, a Hanoi domestic broadcast stated that a letter of condolence had been received upon the death of Nguyen Chi Thanh. It also came from the Central Committee of the PPL and was signed "Secretary General Kaysone Phomvihan."

On October 12, 1967, the Central Committee of the Bulgarian Communist party announced that it had sent a telegram to the Central Committee of the People's party of Laos on the twenty-first anniversary of the proclamation of Lao independence. Later that same year, on December 9, Tirana International Service stated in English that on the occasion of the twenty-third anniversary of Albania's liberation, the Central Committee of the Albanian Workers party had received "greetings from Kaysone Phomvihan, general secretary of the People's Party of Laos."

On March 22, 1968, the East German Communist organ NEUES DEUTSCHLAND, discussing plans for the Budapest consultative meeting of Communist parties, stated that a number of "Marxist-Leninist parties born since 1960" should be invited to participate. Among those parties we find listed the People's Party of Laos (together with the People's Revolutionary Party of Cambodia). Still another reference to the PPL appeared in the summer of 1968 in the Polish Communist press.

On December 2, 1968, upon the occasion of the twenty-fourth anniversary of Albania's liberation, a telegram was received from Kaysone Phomvihan, secretary of the People's Party of Laos.

More recently, on October 10, 1969, the East German NEUES DEUTSCHLAND announced that it had received a message of congratulations on the twentieth anniversary of the founding of the German Democratic Republic. The message conveyed "friendship and militant solidarity between our two parties," and was signed at "San Neua, for the Central Committee of the People's Party of Laos by Kaysone Phomvihan, Secretary General." On the same occasion, the East Berlin ADN Domestic Service reported, on October 9, a message from Prince Souphanouvong, chairman of the Lao Patriotic Front.

17. Pathet Lao News Agency in English, October 5, 1970.

18. For an analysis of the Pathet Lao's relations with the two major Communist powers, see Paul F. Langer, THE SOVIET UNION, CHINA AND THE PATHET LAO: ANALYSIS AND CHRONOLOGY, P-4765, Rand Corporation, Santa Monica, January 1972.

19. The discussion that follows draws heavily upon an authoritative statement of the Lao Dong party: THIRTY YEARS OF STRUGGLE OF THE PARTY, a party history written in commemoration of the thirtieth anniversary of the founding of the Indochinese Communist party, now the Vietnam Lao Dong party. The lessons and experiences of the Vietnamese revolution can be read as relevant to Laos, since, in the words of the study, "they make a contribution to the enrichment of the treasure of revolutionary theory in a colonial and semi-feudal country, in an epoch when imperialism is in decay and socialism is victorious" (p. 102).

20. Truong Chinh's quotation of Ho is found in "President Ho Chi Minh, Revered Leader of the Vietnamese People" (Hanoi, 1966), p. 15, as quoted by Lacouture, HO CHI MINH, p. 47.

21. See Wilfred Burchett, SECOND INDOCHINA WAR (New York: International Publishers, 1970), pp. 93-94, for his description of each of these revolutionary leaders.

22. Pathet Lao News Agency in English, October 5, 1970.

23. This is a 40-page pamphlet printed at the "NLHS Central Printing Office" in 1963.

24. Several documents in our collection confirm this general analysis; for example, LP-9, SAV-12.

25. Pathet Lao News Agency in English, October 5, 1970.

26. This is a 103-page, printed Lao document containing a relatively complicated class analysis, by Lao standards.

27. Anna Louise Strong, CASH AND VIOLENCE IN LAOS (Peking: New World Press, 1961).

28. These statements appear in an article by Kaysone Phomvihan, secretary-general of the PPL, written on the occasion of the twenty-fifth anniversary of the Lao proclamation of independence (October 12, 1945). Pathet Lao News Agency in English, October 5, 1970. For a further authoritative discussion of PPL doctrine, see Phoumi Vongvichit, LAOS AND THE VICTORIOUS STRUGGLE OF THE LAO PEOPLE AGAINST U.S. NEO-COLONIALISM (n.p.: Neo Lao Haksat Editions, 1969).

29. Pathet Lao News Agency in English, October 5, 1970 (FBIS, October 6, 1970).

30. Franz Schurmann, IDEOLOGY AND ORGANIZATION IN COMMUNIST CHINA (Berkeley and Los Angeles: University of California Press, 1968), p. 107.

31. For a description of Captain Hap, and for his testimony on other subjects, see Langer and Zasloff, NORTH VIETNAM AND THE PATHET LAO, Chapter 8, pp. 129-50.

32. Source cited in footnote 12.

33. Asked to define capitalists, according to PL standards, he said: "They classified as capitalists the people who didn't earn their living from their own labor. For example, those who received salaries or worked in an office, the merchants, and the "thao khoun," the administrative authorities at the tasseng level during French rule were capitalists."

34. See Robert Scalapino, ed., THE COMMUNIST REVOLUTION IN ASIA, rev. ed. (Englewood Cliffs, N.J.: Prentice-Hall, 1969), pp. 10, 14-15.

35. Documents cited in above: LP-24, LBN-50, LBN-64, LBN-47, LBN-63, LBN-49.

36. The books, all printed in Laos by Chanthy, editor of the NLHS newspaper at the time, were: THE HISTORY OF MARXISM-LENINISM, edited by Sisana Sisane; THE HISTORY OF THE PPL, by Kaysone Phomvihan with a preface by Khamma; HOW TO APPLY FOR MEMBERSHIP IN THE PPL, by Kaysone Phomvihan (students were instructed not to show this book to any one other than members of the PPL); and LOYALTY, SPEECH AND COMMON OBJECTIVES, by Kaysone Phomvihan and edited by Thongsavat Khaykhamphi-toun. This last book discussed the inaccuracy of common beliefs and superstitions held by those who did not understand the modern world, and instructed the reader that the spirits in which he may believe do not exist.

37. S.T. Hosmer, based upon his examination of PRP documents from South Vietnam, has pointed out this similarity. See S.T. Hosmer, VIET CONG REPRESSION (Lexington, Mass.: Lexington Books, D.C. Heath & Co., 1970).

38. Pathet Lao News Agency in English, October 5, 1970.

39. Our earlier study, NORTH VIETNAM AND THE PATHET LAO, provides ample evidence of North Vietnamese advice and support to the total Pathet Lao movement. In our discussion of North Vietnamese support to the PPL in the following pages, we shall draw particularly upon the notebook of the North Vietnamese economic cadre and upon the testimony of former North Vietnamese Captain Mai Dai Hap, both previously mentioned herein. In addition, we shall refer to a thirteen-page report by Edwin T. McKeithen, "The Role of North Vietnamese Cadres in the PL Administration of Xieng Khouang Province," U.S. Agency for International Development, Vientiane, Laos, April 19. McKeithen is a U.S. AID officer who interviewed refugees who fled from PL-controlled areas in Xieng Khouang Province during 1969.

40. McKeithen, "The Role of North Vietnamese Cadres," p. 4.

41. Pathet Lao News Agency in English, October 5, 1970.

Chapter 3
Politics and Administration

1. UNSERE ZEIT (Essen), June 27, 1970, as translated in Joint Publications Research Service (J.P.R.S.) 51,104 of August 6, 1970.

2. The fronts in South Vietnam, North Vietnam, and Laos are similar in conception. A document of the National Liberation Front of South Vietnam,

showing the likeness of that front to the Lien Viet front in North Vietnam, may be compared with the NLHS document cited above: "In 1941 the Viet Minh was established to lead all our people so that the August Revolution might be crowned with success. During the Resistance period the Lien Viet Front united all our people in a successful resistance. In the present political struggle the National Liberation Front of South Vietnam is in charge of leading the South Vietnam population in struggling successfully for the liberation of South Vietnam and carrying out the unification of our country. The operational plans of the Front . . . aim at serving the supreme interests of the Fatherland and at meeting the urgent and present aspirations of the South Vietnam population." Cited in Douglas Pike, VIET CONG (Cambridge, Mass.: M.I.T. Press, 1966), p. 81.

3. George Krausz, VON INDIEN BIS LAOS (Berlin, 1960), pp. 327-29; our translation from the German.

4. For a discussion of this Vietnamese Communist front policy, see Jeffrey Race, "How They Won," ASIAN SURVEY, August 1970, pp. 628-50. Race has provided the following translation of a Vietnamese Communist regional committee document dated January 1961, entitled "Instructions to Zones 1, 2, 3, 4" (Eastern, Central, and Western Zones of Nam-Bo and the Saigon-Cholon Special Zone), which clearly puts forth this policy. Race notes that a photograph of this document is contained in A THREAT TO PEACE, published by the U.S. Department of State in 1961.

Naturally among these classes [composing the Front] only the working class occupies the vanguard leadership role. The alliance of the workers and peasants is the basic force composing the Front, because these two classes make up the absolute majority of the Front's numbers and moreover have the most resolute and self-sacrificing spirit. However, in the present realistic situation in the South, these two classes do not have the capability of achieving decisive victories for the revolution.

For this reason the Central Committee has developed a front policy and established the National Liberation Front, in order to attract the bourgeoisie and the intellectuals, including the urban students and youths, and the middle and rich peasants in the countryside. In their speeches at the Third Party Congress, Comrades Le Duan and Le Duc Tho stated their judgments that urban youths, students, intellectuals and bourgeoisie in the South, and the rural middle and rich peasants, although possessing a [progressive] spirit and political awareness, are easily turned into opponents of the socialist revolution and of Marxism-Leninism and easily develop a passive self-serving attitude. Nevertheless, in the present situation in the South, the Central Committee believes it necessary to do everything possible to attract these elements into the Front. In this the Central Committee is not betraying the class line of the Party and the revolution, nor will the Central Committee entrust important revolutionary responsibilities to these elements. This step is taken only to exploit to the fullest the capabilities and the standing of these elements, in order to advance the revolution and to add to the standing of the National Liberation Front. This policy is a temporary strategy of the Party. When the revolution is victorious, it will be revised and at that time we will act openly, and assume leadership of the revolution.

This translation is found in Race's discussion paper, "How They Won," for a Conference of the Southeast Asia Development Advisory Group (SEADAG) held at the Asia House, New York City, on June 23, 1969.

5. See Anita L. Nutt, TROIKA ON TRIAL—CONTROL OR COMPROMISE (U.S. Department of Defense, 1967), for a discussion of PL and Viet Minh regroupment in the two provinces.

6. See Appendix B for membership of the Central Committee in 1950 and 1956.

7. It is interesting that the new statutes were copied almost verbatim from the constitution of the Vietnam Fatherland front which had been reorganized in North Vietnam only a year earlier. Embarrassment at the disclosure of this resemblance, and pressure from the RLG ministry of the interior, to whom the statutes were passed for registration, caused certain changes to be made in the language. See ASIAN NOTES, No. 16, April 24, 1964.

8. The CDNI, according to former Assistant Secretary of State Roger Hilsman, was formed with the encouragement and assistance of the American CIA. See TO MOVE A NATION (Garden City, New York: Doubleday & Co., Inc., 1967), pp. 114-15.

9. In addition to the seven Assemblymen mentioned in the text as elected in May 1958, the others arrested were: Singkapo Chounramany, Mune, Phao Thiaphachano, Khamphet Phommavan, Ma Khaikhamphithoun, Bouasy, Phoukheo Vanamphay, (Maha) Boumboun, and Mana.

10. See Appendix C for ten-point program.

11. See Appendix B for list of the new Central Committee.

12. FBIS, November 16, 1968.

13. See Appendix D for the twelve-point program.

14. Richard E. Ward, "PL Hole Up in Caves, Where Prince Sees Press," WASHINGTON POST, August 2, 1970. Ward, who travelled through North Vietnam and Communist-controlled areas in Laos from May 22 through June, 1950, is foreign affairs editor of THE GUARDIAN, a radical weekly published in New York City. His description of the cave facilities in Sam Neua accords with reports we have seen by French, Soviet, and East European journalists, most of whom were received by Souphanouvong.

15. In 1963, a group led by Colonel Deuane Souvannaroth and closely affiliated with the Pathet Lao split away from the Kong Le forces on the Plain of Jars. They have since referred to themselves as the "True Patriotic Neutralists" while the "Kong Le Neutralists" are said to have become "lackeys of the American imperialists." Another group led by Khammouane Boupha who is a powerful figure in Phong Saly Province, an area surrounded by Chinese, North Vietnamese, and Pathet Lao control, found it expedient to ally themselves with the Pathet Lao. These two groups are loosely affiliated and are often referred to by RLG authorities as "Dissident Neutralists."

16. Xieng Mouan and others, THE WOOD GROUSE (N.p.: Neo Lao Haksat Publications, 1968), p. 34.

17. Pathet Lao broadcast, February 13, 1968.

18. See Appendix G for a sample list of these PL organizations.

19. Statements for foreign consumption are frequently issued from NLHS central headquarters in the name of one of these associations. For example, the Pathet Lao Radio, broadcasting in English on April 10, 1969, announced that the Laotian Patriotic Youth League had sent a message to the National Coordination Committee To End the War in Vietnam and to the Students for Democratic Society (SDS), expressing "high indignation at the Washington authorities for having arrested eight American peace militants."

20. FBIS, November 16, 1965.

21. Described in a report by Edwin T. McKeithen, LIFE UNDER THE PL IN XIENG KHOUANG VILLE AREA (U.S. Agency for International Development, Vientiane, Laos, July 10, 1969), pp. 6-7.

22. WORTHY DAUGHTERS AND SONS OF THE LAO PEOPLE (NLHS Publications), pp. 55-56.

23. RAINS IN THE JUNGLE (NLHS Publications, 1967), p. 39.

24. See McKeithen, LIFE UNDER THE PL.

25. Report of interview with refugees from former PL-held areas near Muong Phine, in Savannakhet Province, by R.L. Spencer, United States Information Service (USIS), Savannakhet, Laos, September 15, 1969.

26. From a document dated July 29, 1965.

27. For earlier information on the Lao refugee problem, see hearings before the U.S. Senate Committee of Judiciary, Subcommittee to Investigate Problems Connected with Refugees, and Escapees, REFUGEE AND CIVILIAN WAR CASUALTY PROBLEMS IN LAOS AND CAMBODIA, 91st Congress, 2nd Session, May 7, 1970; also REFUGEE AND CIVILIAN WAR CASUALTY PROBLEMS IN INDOCHINA, a staff report of this subcommittee, 91st Congress, 2nd Session, September 28, 1970.

28. McKeithen, LIFE UNDER THE PL, pp. 17-18.

29. Edwin T. McKeithen, "The Role of North Vietnamese Cadres in the PL Administration in Xieng Khouang Province," U.S. Agency for International Development, Vientiane, Laos, April 1970, p. 1.

30. This is the view of the U.S. State Department, as reflected in testimony before Senator Edward Kennedy's committee investigating refugees. The department's statement pointed out that hill-tribe resentment is diminishing as minority groups are accepted for civil service posts. See hearings before the(Senator Kennedy) Subcommittee, Refugee and Civilian War Casualty Problems, p. 69.

Chapter 4
The Pathet Lao Fighting Forces

1. An article entitled "Pathet Lao Fighting Units—The 13th Anniversary of an Army of Patriots," PEKING REVIEW, February 2, 1962, relates the story of

the beginnings of the Pathet Lao military forces in these words: "The Pathet Lao Fighting Units came into being when the Laotian people were fighting against the French colonialists. On January 20, 1949, two guerrilla detachments in Sam Neua, the old revolutionary base in Laos, merged and took the name of Lat Savong, after an 18th century national hero who rendered distinguished service to his country when fighting back a Siamese invasion. The first detachment of the Pathet Lao Fighting Units was made up of 25 poorly equipped and inadequately supplied men."

2. Radio Pathet Lao in Lao, October 11, 1965. See also Wilfred Burchett, MEKONG UPSTREAM (Hanoi: Red River Publishing House, 1957), pp. 286-88, for an account reflecting the PL official history.

3. La documentation française, LE LAOS, Notes et Etudes Documentaires, No. 3630, 20 October 1969, p. 16.

4. According to Arthur J. Dommen, CONFLICT IN LAOS, New York: Praeger Publishers, Revised Edition, 1971, p. 86.

5. For the structure of the North Vietnamese and PL forces, as of September 1969, see U.S. SECURITY AGREEMENTS AND COMMITMENTS ABROAD, Kingdom of Thailand hearings before the Subcommittee on U.S. Security Agreements Abroad, Committee on Foreign Relations, U.S. Senate, 91st Congress, 1st Session, Part 3, (hereafter, Thailand hearings), p. 715, and the same committee's Kingdom of Laos hearings of October 1969 (hereafter, Laos hearings), pp. 373-74.

6. See Laos hearings, p. 495.

7. See Laos hearings, pp. 489-90; and testimony by Ambassador William H. Sullivan at hearings before the U.S. Senate Committee of Judiciary, Subcommittee to Investigate Problems Connected with Refugees and Escapees, REFUGEE AND CIVILIAN WAR CASUALTY PROBLEMS IN LAOS AND CAMBODIA, 91st Congress, 2nd Session, May 7, 1970 (hereafter, Refugee hearings), p. 61.

8. Laos hearings, p. 490.

9. WASHINGTON EVENING STAR, June 25 and June 29, 1969.

10. In the huge cache of supplies and weapons captured by General Vang Pao's troops in the Plain of Jars offensive of September 1969 were sixteen Soviet PD-76 tanks, part of the Communist force of some sixty tanks which had been provided by Soviet assistance during 1961 and 1962 to Pathet Lao and Kong Le forces on the Plain of Jars. See testimony by U.S. Military Attaché Colonel Duskin, Laos hearings, pp. 492-93.

11. Stanley Karnow, WASHINGTON POST, August 16, 1969; Arbuckle, WASHINGTON EVENING STAR, August 20, 1969. For discussion of the U.S. air role in Laos, see Laos hearings, especially pp. 456-70; also Refugee hearings, pp. 47-48. For figures on 1970 and 1971 U.S. air sorties, see THAILAND, LAOS AND CAMBODIA: JANUARY 1972. A Staff Report Prepared for the Use of the Subcommittee on U.S. Security Agreements and Commitments Abroad of the Committee on Foreign Relations, U.S. Senate, May 8, 1972, pp. 14-15.

12. NEW YORK TIMES, October 11, 1969.

13. WASHINGTON EVENING STAR, August 22, 1969.

14. Refugee hearings, p. 63. The following tabulation, showing the number of refugees on the RLG side in Laos recorded by the U.S. AID agency, was submitted to the subcommittee. Figures for 1969 and 1970 are based on a rounded number of 100,000 for those aided by the U.S. Department of Defense.

1966 -	August	147,500
1967 -	February	130,400
	August	158,800
1968 -	February	136,900
	August	128,200
1969 -	February	157,000
	April	187,000
	May	198,000
	June	206,000
	July	225,000
	August	232,000
	September	242,000
	October-November	250,000
	December	235,000
1970 -	January	204,000
	February	204,000
	March	204,000
	April	246,000

15. We have examined training documents that show relatively sophisticated instructions to soldiers for defense against air attacks. The general population, too, are provided guidance from cadres for dealing with the bombings. The following excerpt from a Lao radio broadcast offers a sample of their messages to the public:

Our parents and all organizations must form their own groups to work in shifts and to survey the movements of enemy spies, who spot for air raids. Any movement or encampment must be camouflaged to blend with its surroundings. When they hear the noise of U.S. aircraft they must inform or signal to one another immediately in order to avoid destruction. They must act in accordance with discipline of their own battalions or regiments when they cook or dry their uniforms in the sun. They should make a fire without smoke. All bridges and landing places must be repaired for use at any time, so that U.S. aircraft can never completely destroy them. Our parents, children, and teachers must form groups to keep them in good condition and repair any damage due to U.S. air raids. Furthermore, we must establish local medical units to help wounded people when they are hit by U.S. bombs and bullets and at the same time they must establish mobile engineering units to repair roads and bridges in timely fashion.

Radio Pathet Lao in Lao, February 5, 1968.

16. Radio Pathet Lao in English, July 24, 1969.

17. Pathet Lao News Agency in English, October 12, 1970.

18. Thailand hearings, p. 715.

19. See testimony of the former U.S. Army Attaché Representative in Luang Prabang, Major Robert W. Thomas, in October 1969, at the Laos hearings, p. 552.

20. Edwin T. McKeithen, LIFE UNDER THE PL IN XIENG KHOUANG VILLE AREA, U.S. Agency for International Development, Vientiane, Laos, July 10, 1969, pp. 18-19.

21. FBIS, February 21, 1968.

22. VOIX DU LAOS, April 24, 1967.

23. Hanoi, VNA International Service in English, June 15, 1967.

24. FBIS, October 26, 1968.

25. PHOUKOUT STRONGHOLD, 1967, p. 21. Another collection of stories by Xieng Mouan and others, THE WOOD GROUSE (N.p.: Neo Lao Haksat Publications, 1968), also contains references to women guerrillas.

26. Radio Pathet Lao in Lao, December 3, 1969; FBIS, December 11, 1969.

27. FBIS, April 23, 1968.

28. Radio Pathet Lao in Lao, October 22, 1969; FBIS, October 29, 1969.

29. Ibid.

30. Pathet Lao News Agency in English; FBIS, December 4, 1970.

31. Radio Pathet Lao in Lao, FBIS, July 18, 1969.

32. Radio Pathet Lao in Lao, July 9, 1969; FBIS, July 15, 1969.

33. Following are the guides to proper behavior published by the LPLA propaganda and training section:

8 Rules of the LPLA

Obey orders of superiors at all times.

Do not take public property.

Observe good sanitation. Do not foul the well, the latrine area, or other public places.

Show respect for seniors and women, and affection for children.

Do not take even a single needle or a piece of thread from the people without payment. Return anything you borrow; replace anything you lose.

Make propaganda, teach the people, and help them with their work.

Show respect for traditions; tolerate all religions; respect temples and other sacred buildings.

Keep secrecy about military movements and revolutionary activities.

8 Oaths of the LPLA

Sacrifice everything for the revolution and struggle against the American imperialists and their lackeys to restore peace, independence, sovereignty, unity and stability to the nation.

Place full confidence in the leadership of the Party. Absolutely follow the orders of superiors. Maintain good discipline and carry out all assignments.

Be diligent in learning; show a good example in your work; be vigilant against tricks of the enemy; persevere in the face of difficulty; refuse temptations of money, beauty, and pleasure.

Do not reveal secrets. Remain loyal to the revolution if captured and tortured by the enemy.

Keep weapons and equipment in good condition and do not let them be seized by the enemy, even if it means death.

Be harmonious with members of the army. Live together and help one another as members of the same family.

Abide by these three maxims in dealing with the people:

> Respect the people of all nationalities; protect the lives and property of the people; do not threaten, cause trouble, or take property without consent from the people.

Make this slogan come true: The army and the people are of the same heart and the armed forces are to the people as fish to water.

Encourage self-improvement and inclination to revolution. Refrain from anything that would damage the reputation of the army and the Lao nation.

12 Rules for Dealing with the People

4 Respects

Respect and treat people of all ethnic groups as father, mother, brother and sister of the same family.

Respect the traditions of people of all ethnic groups.

Respect the beliefs of the people, the monks, and clergy.

Respect and support the local administration.

4 Don't's

Don't beat, threaten, or swear at the people.

Don't take any property from the people without permission.

Don't destroy temples, churches or public property.

Don't take liberties with girls.

4 Helps

Help people earn their living, improve their production, and repair their houses.

Help educate the people about politics and culture.

Help the people improve their sanitation and give them medical aid when necessary.

Help the people fight against the enemy for the defense of the country.

LP-14. These rules and oaths were first taught to PL soldiers in January 1949, according to a weekly political talk series on Radio PL in Lao, November 12, 1969, FBIS, November 19, 1969.

34. PHOUKOUT STRONGHOLD, p. 17.

35. Radio Pathet Lao in Lao, July 30, 1969; FBIS, August 8, 1969.

36. Radio Pathet Lao in Lao, August 27, 1969; FBIS, September 4, 1969.

37. Chalmers Johnson describes the Communist Chinese practice in the following manner: "During 1960 and 1961, the Army undertook the "two-remembrances and three-inspections" movement, the "four-good company" movement and the "five-good soldier" movement. The two-remembrances were of class difficulties and of national difficulties; the three things to inspect were one's viewpoint, one's fighting spirit, and one's work. The four-good company movement consisted of good political ideology, good military training, good "three-eight style," and good personal discipline. The five-good soldiers movement consisted of good political thought, good productive labor, good results of study, good military and political activities, and good organization and discipline." "Building a Communist Nation in China," in Robert A. Scalapino, ed., THE COMMUNIST REVOLUTION IN ASIA, rev. ed. (Englewood Cliffs, N.J.: Prentice-Hall, 1969), p. 59.

38. Radio Pathet Lao broadcast from San Neua, October 20, 1970.

39. Radio Pathet Lao broadcast of October 22, 1970.

40. See, for example, Xieng Mouan, p. 63.

Appendix A
Background and Profiles of Pathet Lao Leaders

1. CAMBODIA AND LAOS FIGHT HAND IN HAND WITH VIETNAM FOR FREEDOM (N.p.: Vietnam Central Information Service, April 1951). Giving prominence to the eastern group of the Lao resistance movement, this publication states that "at the end of 1947, the political situation in Thailand becoming unfavorable to the Laos revolution, all forces in Western Laos shifted and concentrated in Eastern Laos to create resistance bases in the Eastern part of South Laos" (p. 18). Since the Viet Minh played a major role in the developing Lao resistance organization in eastern Laos, while exerting a relatively minor influence upon the group in Thailand, it is not surprising that this Viet Minh publication emphasizes the Lao resistance in the east. In fact, the Lao exiles in Thailand continued, until 1949, to represent the major segment of the Lao nationalist movement.

2. The first chairman of that committee, who also commanded several hundred Lao guerrilla troops in southern Laos, claimed that Nouhak opposed his ties to the Issara government in Thailand and sent agents to challenge his leadership. According to this official, Phoumi Nosavan, who was allied with Nouhak at the time, and others including Singkapo brought troops to challenge him. Nouhak used his contacts with the Viet Minh commanders to overthrow this commander's authority. Reference is made to these guerrilla units in the Viet Minh publication, CAMBODIA AND LAO FIGHT HAND IN HAND WITH VIETNAM, op. cit., p. 17.

3. Arthur J. Dommen, CONFLICT IN LAOS (New York: Praeger Publishers, Revised Edition, 1964), p. 75.

4. A Communist author who interviewed him in 1957 gave the following account of Faydang's joining the Lao resistance movement: "I heard there had been a great battle in Thakhek and that the townspeople had fought very bravely against the French. I thought it would be very good if we could fight together against the same enemy. I went down to the plains myself and tried to find this prince. He had already left and was in Thailand. I sent him a message and the reply came back: "Arouse the people. Create a strong organization. Later we will fight together." So I returned to the mountains and began to organize all the [Meo] villagers from our own base . . . every village appointed organizers and formed scouts and defense corps." Wilfred Burchett, MEKONG UPSTREAM (Hanoi: Red River Publishing House, 1957), p. 264.

While Faydang may have had contacts with Prince Souphanouvong in 1946, this 1957 interview sounds suspiciously like a public relations release supporting Souphanouvong, the incumbent spokesman of the Pathet Lao in 1957, rather than accurate history. Faydang's organizational links were with the Committee of Resistance in the East in 1946, not with the Issara in Thailand, which was Souphanouvong's base at the time. It seems more likely that the Viet Minh established contact with Faydang and urged him to organize his resistance effort, later called the Meo Resistance League.

5. Burchett, MEKONG UPSTREAM, p. 257.

6. La documentation française, LE LAOS, Notes et Etudes Documentaires, No. 3630, 20 Octobre 1969, p. 13.

7. Burchett, MEKONG UPSTREAM, p. 257.

8. It must be recalled that Giap was then a teacher in North Vietnam. Dommen (CONFLICT IN LAOS, p. 73), reports that Ho Chi Minh sent Kaysone to Savannakhet in 1945 with the mission to infiltrate a Lao nationalist movement that had been organized by Oun Sananikone, the "Greater Laos" (Lao Pen Lao) movement (Dommen, p. 73). It is not clear what role Kaysone had in this movement, if any, but, in any case, the organization petered out.

9. Dommen, CONFLICT IN LAOS, p. 73.

10. See Hugh Toye, LAOS: BUFFER STATE OR BATTLEGROUND (London and New York: Oxford University Press, 1968).

11. An interview with General Singkapo, which confirms these biographical details, was published in the Rumanian newspaper LUMEA, September 17, 1970, pp. 19-20. A translation is in Joint Publications Research Service (JPRS) 51826, No. 274, November 20, 1970, translation of South and East Asia, pp. 7-11. Souphanouvong, in a letter to the Issara government, claimed that Singkapo acted cowardly in the Thakhek battle against the French in 1946. The letter was in the collection of documents of the late Nhouy Abhay. Excerpts from the letters by Souphanouvong in the collection are quoted in Paul F. Langer and Joseph J. Zasloff, NORTH VIETNAM AND THE PATHET LAO (Cambridge, Mass.: Harvard University Press, 1970), pp. 23-45.

12. See ibid, pp. 224-25, for a partial list of the participants at this congress.

13. CAMBODIA AND LAOS FIGHT HAND IN HAND WITH VIETNAM.

14. For further accounts, see BANGKOK POST, January 3, 1969; LE MONDE, January 2, 1969; UPI release, December 31, 1968.

15. A Pathet Lao News Agency report of October 2, 1969, stated that Kaysone participated in a meeting of the NLHS standing committee which was held from September 25 to 27 under Souphanouvong's chairmanship.

16. While Lao membership in the ICP and the Lao Dong party was plausible, and reports of PL members in these two parties come from persons who purport to have a personal knowledge, we have found no way to confirm these claims and simply report them as credible.

17. Hanoi broadcast in Vietnamese, FBIS, July 19, 1967.

18. A successor to Kaysone as director of the Kommadam training school (A-18), who served under Kaysone's command, told us that Kaysone proudly showed him an album with photographs of himself with Ho Chi Minh and Pham Van Dong (now prime minister of North Vietnam) taken in North Vietnam, 1953-54.

19. Although the reasons for Kaysone's decision to run in Attopeu, south of his birthplace, are not clear, there is little reason to believe that as the son of a minor colonial bureaucrat who was Vietnamese (still living in Savannakhet at the time), his political appeal to the lowland Lao in his home town would have been substantial.

20. Later chairman of the DRV National Reunification Committee of the National Assembly, who died on July 28, 1969, at age 69. Hanoi broadcast in English, FBIS, July 31, 1969.

21. Possibly another daughter and a son. His daughter, by his first wife, is now married to a colonel in the FAR (A18).

22. A more complete account of Prince Souphanouvong's early career and nationalist activities is given in Langer and Zasloff, Chapter 3.

Index

Selected Rand Books

Averch, H., et al. THE MATRIX OF POLICY IN THE PHILIPPINES. Princeton, N.J.: Princeton University Press, 1971.

Bagdikian, Ben H. THE INFORMATION MACHINES: THEIR IMPACT ON MEN AND THE MEDIA. New York: Harper and Row, 1971.

Canby, Steven L. MILITARY MANPOWER PROCUREMENT: A POLICY ANALYSIS. Lexington, Mass.: D.C. Heath and Company, 1972.

Clawson, M., et al. THE AGRICULTURAL POTENTIAL OF THE MIDDLE EAST. New York: American Elsevier Publishing Company, 1971.

Coleman, James S. and Nancy L. Karweit. INFORMATION SYSTEMS AND PERFORMANCE MEASURES IN SCHOOLS. Englewood Cliffs, New Jersey: Educational Technology Publications, 1972.

Cooper, Charles A., and Sidney S. Alexander. ECONOMIC DEVELOPMENT AND POPULATION GROWTH IN THE MIDDLE EAST. New York: American Elsevier Publishing Company, 1972.

Dalkey, Norman C. (ed.) STUDIES IN THE QUALITY OF LIFE: DELPHI AND DECISION-MAKING. Lexington, Mass.: D.C. Heath and Company, 1972.

Fisher, Gene H. COST CONSIDERATIONS IN SYSTEMS ANALYSIS. New York: American Elsevier Publishing Company, 1971.

Goldhamer, Herbert. THE FOREIGN POWERS IN LATIN AMERICA. Princeton, N.J.: Princeton University Press, 1972.

Gurtov, Melvin. SOUTHEAST ASIA TOMORROW: PROBLEMS AND PROSPECTS FOR U.S. POLICY. Baltimore, Maryland: The Johns Hopkins Press, 1970.

Hammond, Paul Y. and Sidney S. Alexander. POLITICAL DYNAMICS IN THE MIDDLE EAST. New York: American Elsevier Publishing Company, 1972.

Hosmer, Stephen T. VIET CONG REPRESSION AND ITS IMPLICATIONS FOR THE FUTURE. Lexington, Mass.: D.C. Heath and Company, 1970.

Langer, Paul and Joseph J. Zasloff. NORTH VIETNAM AND THE PATHET LAO: PARTNERS IN THE STRUGGLE FOR LAOS. Cambridge, Mass.: Harvard University Press, 1970.

Leites, Nathan and Charles Wolf, Jr. REBELLION AND AUTHORITY: AN ANALYTIC ESSAY ON INSURGENT CONFLICTS. Chicago, Illinois: Markham Publishing Company, 1970.

Moorsteen, Richard and Morton I. Abramowitz. REMAKING CHINA POLICY: U.S.-CHINA RELATIONS AND GOVERNMENTAL DECISIONMAKING. Cambridge, Mass.: Harvard University Press, 1971.

Nelson, Richard R., T. Paul Schultz, and Robert L. Slighton. STRUCTURAL CHANGE IN A DEVELOPING ECONOMY: COLOMBIA'S PROBLEMS AND PROSPECTS. Princeton, New Jersey: Princeton University Press, 1971.

Quade, Edward S. and Wayne I. Boucher. SYSTEMS ANALYSIS AND POLICY

PLANNING: APPLICATIONS IN DEFENSE. New York: American Elsevier Publishing Company, 1968.

Robinson, Thomas W., et al. THE CULTURAL REVOLUTION IN CHINA. Berkeley, California: University of California Press, 1971.

Schurr, Sam H., et al. MIDDLE EASTERN OIL AND THE WESTERN WORLD: PROSPECTS AND PROBLEMS. New York: American Elsevier Publishing Company, 1971.

Sharpe, William F. THE ECONOMICS OF COMPUTERS. New York: Columbia University Press, 1969.

Stepan, Alfred. THE MILITARY IN POLITICS: CHANGING PATTERNS IN BRAZIL. Princeton, N.J.: Princeton University Press, 1971.

Wolfe, Thomas W. SOVIET POWER AND EUROPE 1945-1970. Baltimore Maryland: The Johns Hopkins Press, 1970.

About the Author

Joseph J. Zasloff received the A.B. and M.L. degrees from the University of Pittsburgh and the Ph.D. in International Relations from the University of Geneva, Switzerland.

In addition to having held teaching appointments in universities both in the United States and throughout Southeast Asia, Dr. Zasloff has done consulting work for The RAND Corporation, AID, the Peace Corps, the United States Air Force and the United Nations in the area of Asian and Southeast Asian relations. He has written numerous articles for scholarly publications and, with Allan E. Goodman, coedited *Indochina in Conflict: A Political Assessment* published by Lexington Books. Dr. Zasloff is currently Professor of Political Science at the University of Pittsburgh.

gris